Published by
Revolutionary Hearts Industries

Illustrated by Naomi Winston

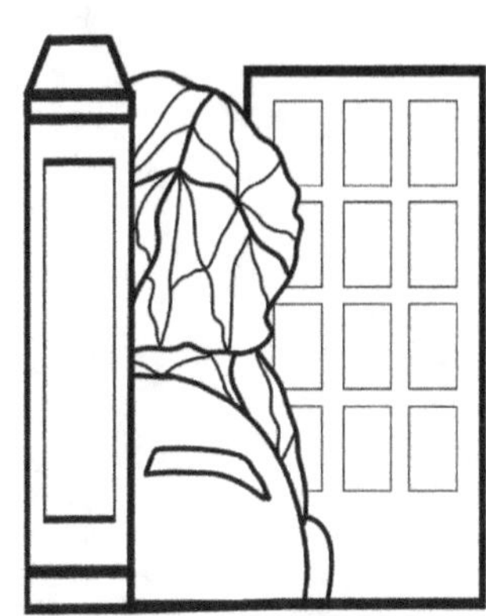

To a beautiful Black girl,

Know that I value you and deeply care about you (so do the rest of the women in this book). Know that you are the reason that I have found purpose in the world.

Know that every single day that I wake up I am dedicated to finding new ways to love you, create space for you, and open doors for you. Know that I truly believe that the world is a better place because you are in it.

Know that I am part of a generation that is creating pathways for you to succeed but also communities for you to heal, grow, and thrive.

Know that you are deeply loved. You are deeply cared for. You are deeply appreciated. You are sincerely needed. I am who I am because of you and what I know you can do in this world. I hope that makes me someone that you can be proud to know. You deserve to live in a world that cares about you. You deserve to be surrounded by a community that values you. You deserve to feel safe.

Know that I will always fight for you and alongside you. Know that I believe in you and all the greatness you hold.
Know with every breath you breathe that I am grateful for your existence.

Remember, that everything has a purpose and you are everything.

LETTER FROM THE AUTHOR

BLACK WOMEN ARE THE FUTURE

"Ain't Nothing More Beautiful than to be a woman and black."

— Naomi Winston

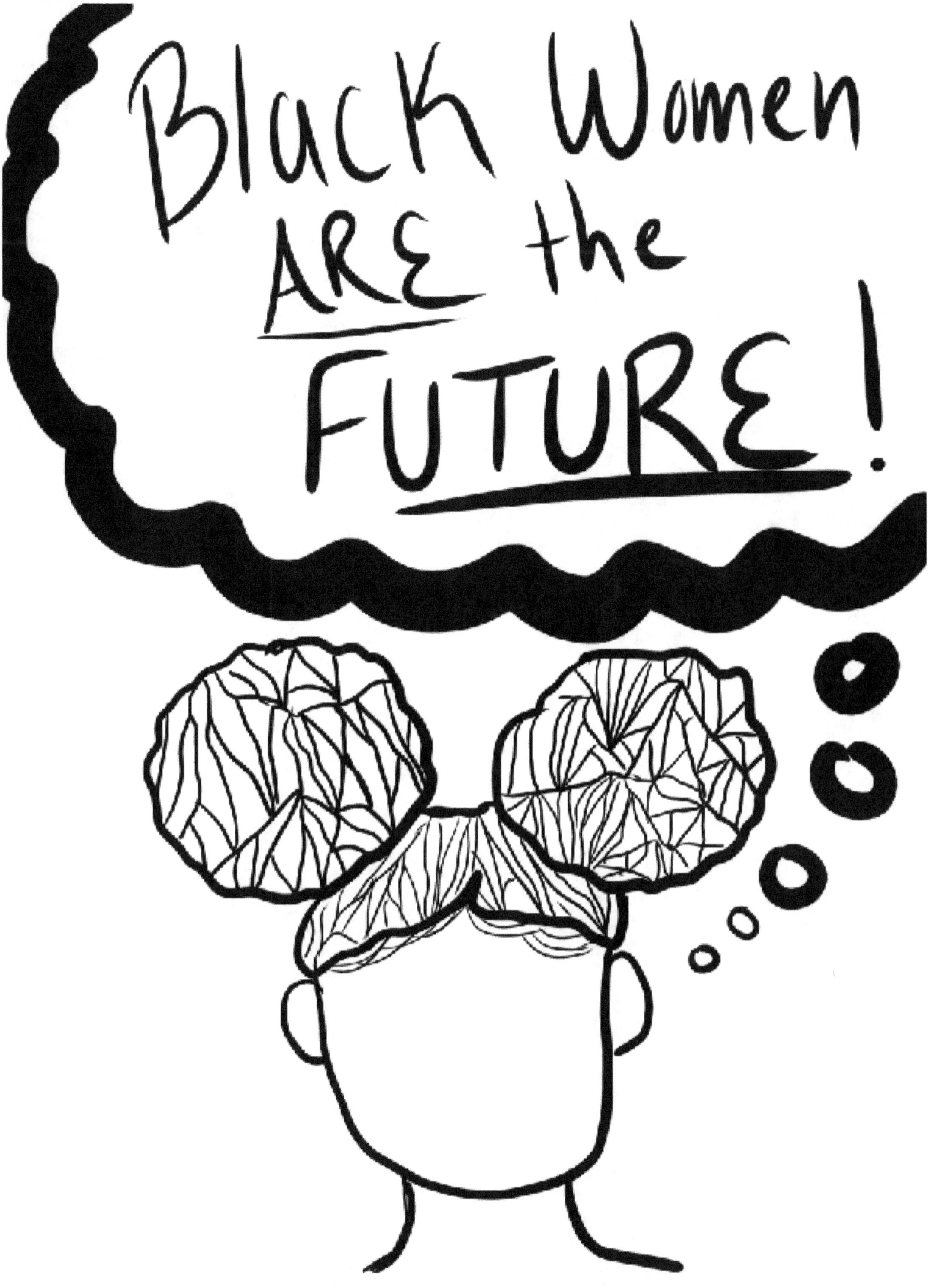

Black Women ARE the FUTURE!

Dedicated to my dad who always made sure I knew I was beautiful

Dedicated to my mom who made sure I knew that I was a powerful black woman

Dedicated to my little cousins because I always want them to know that they are beautiful the way that they are

You are...

You are going to be told a lot of negative things as you live your life. People are going to tell you that you don't belong. People are going to tell you that you are not beautiful, smart, creative, or important enough to be in rooms where you have earned your place. You are worth the world little black girl. You may not understand this now but I hope you hear these words when you are older and remember how amazing you are.

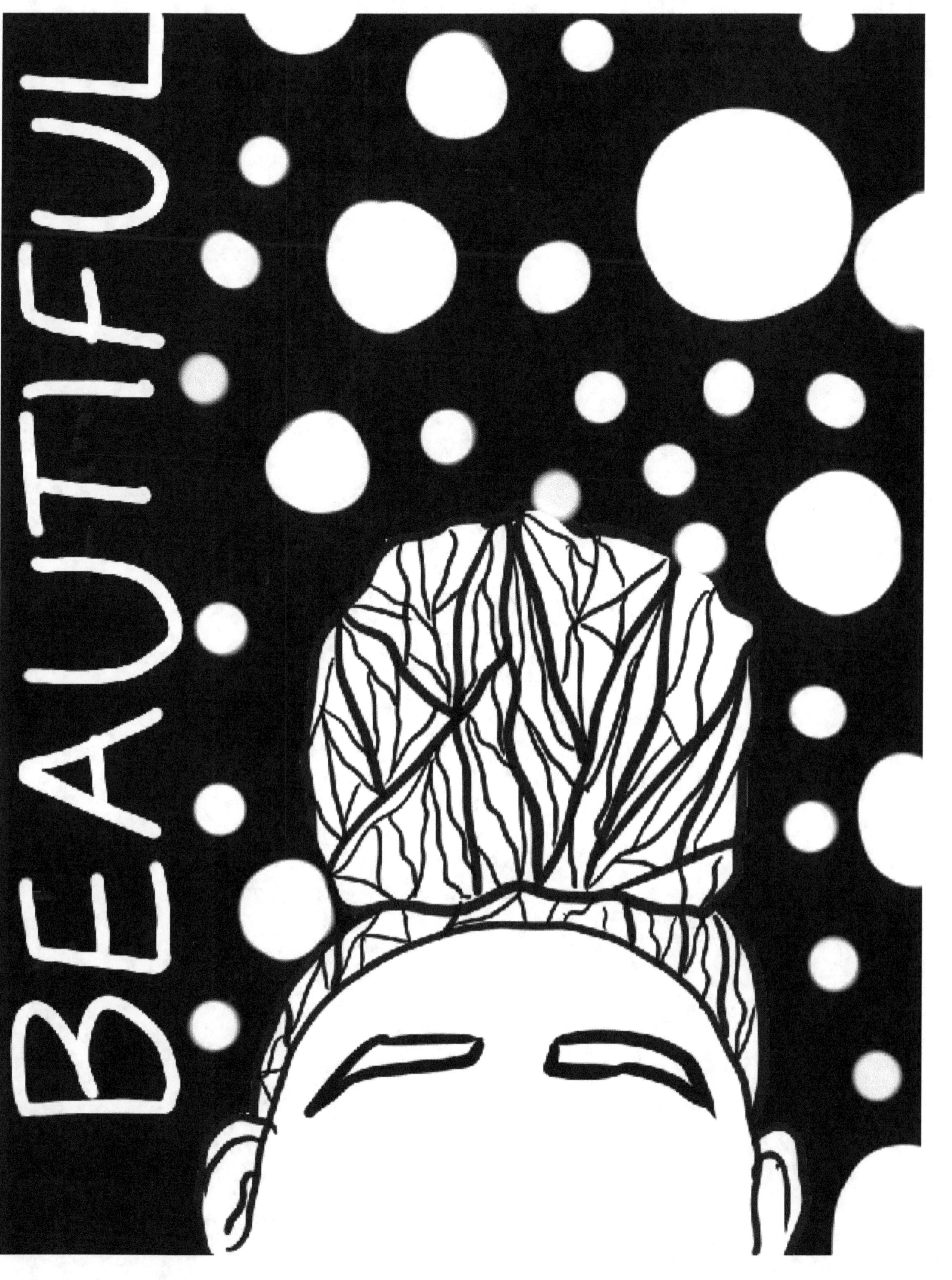

BEAUTIFUL

You are valued.

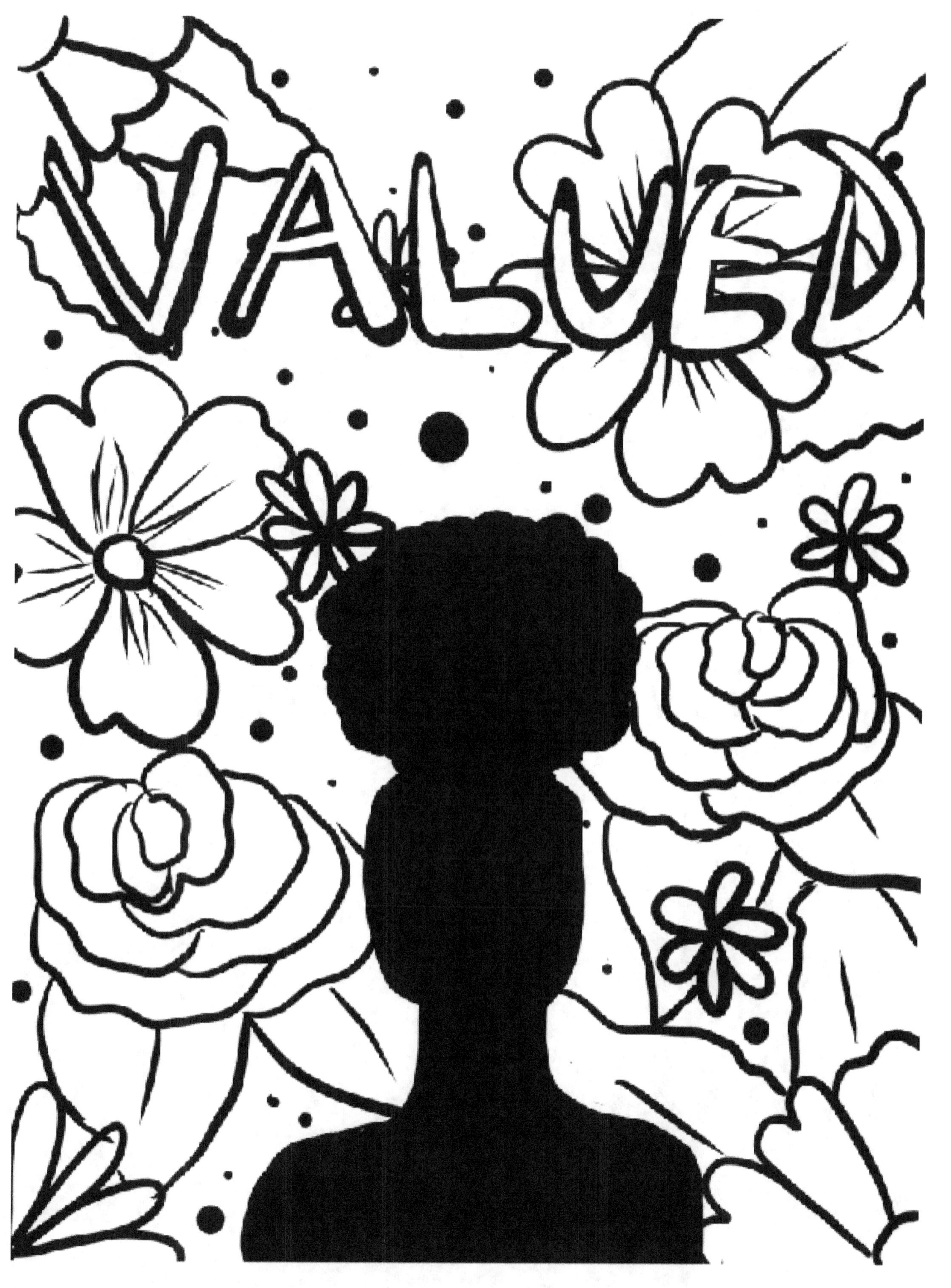
VALUED

You are intelligent.

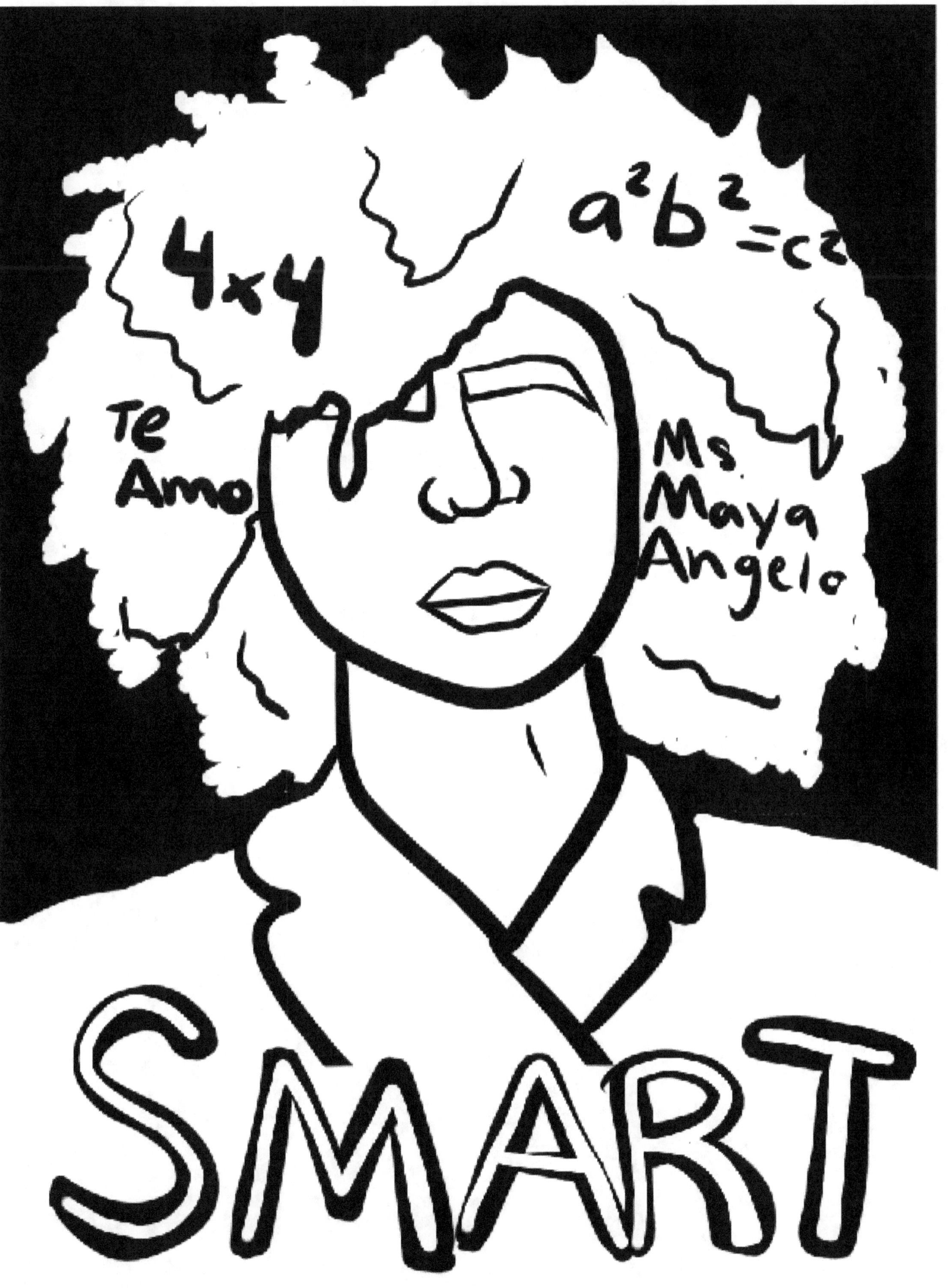

4 x y
a²b² = c²
Te Amo
Ms. Maya Angelo
SMART

You deserve respect.

MATTER

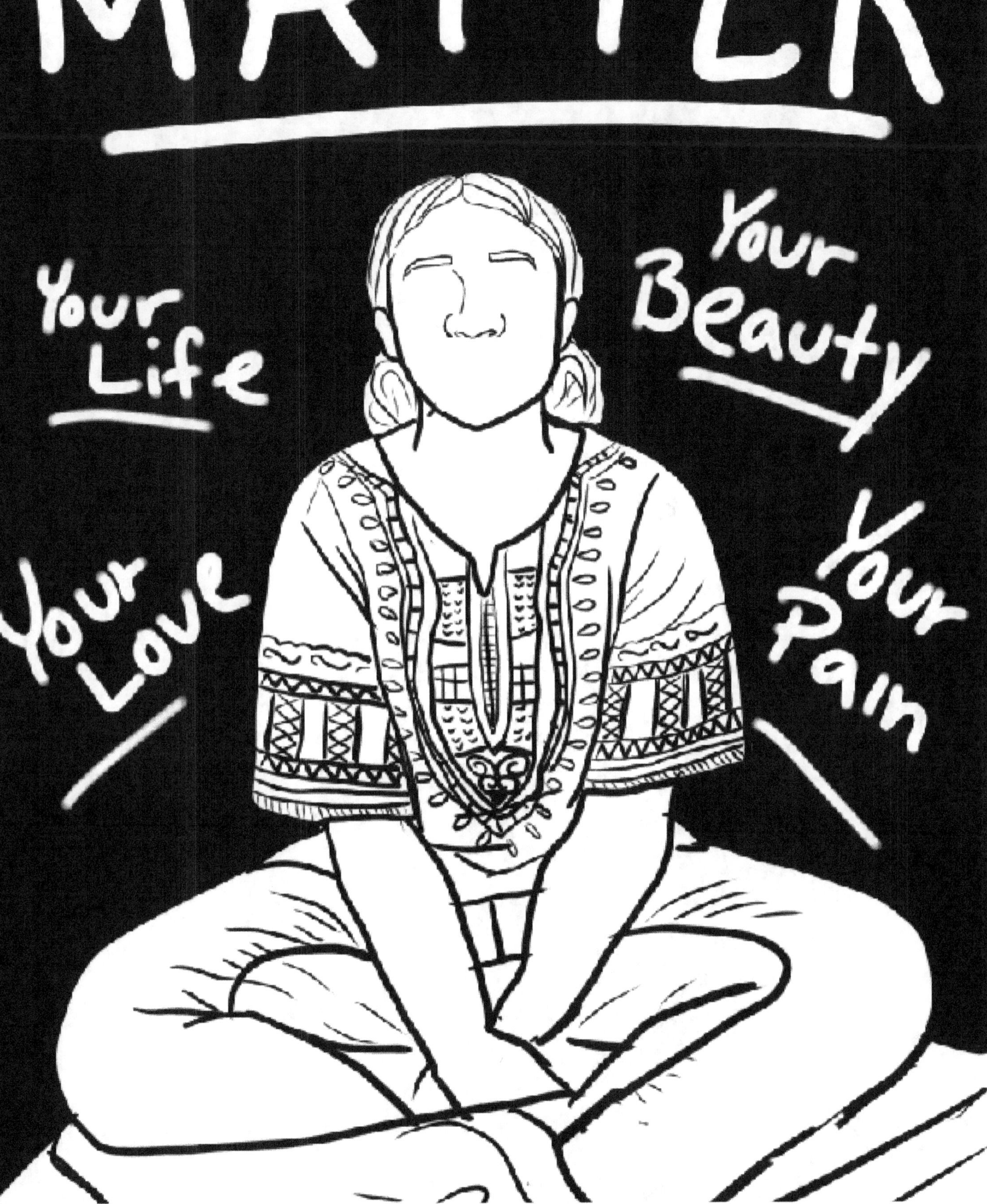

You deserve happiness.

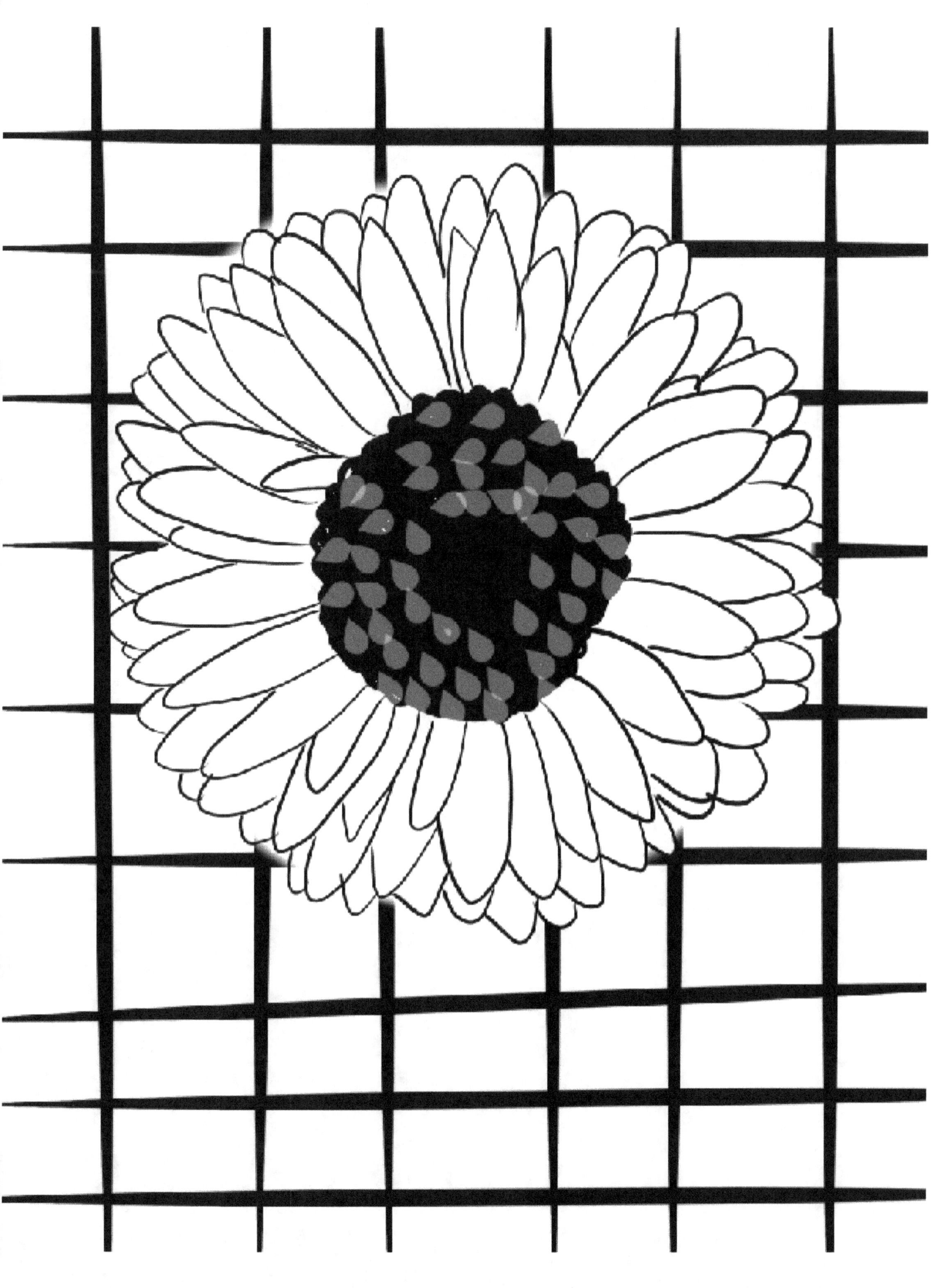

You are important.

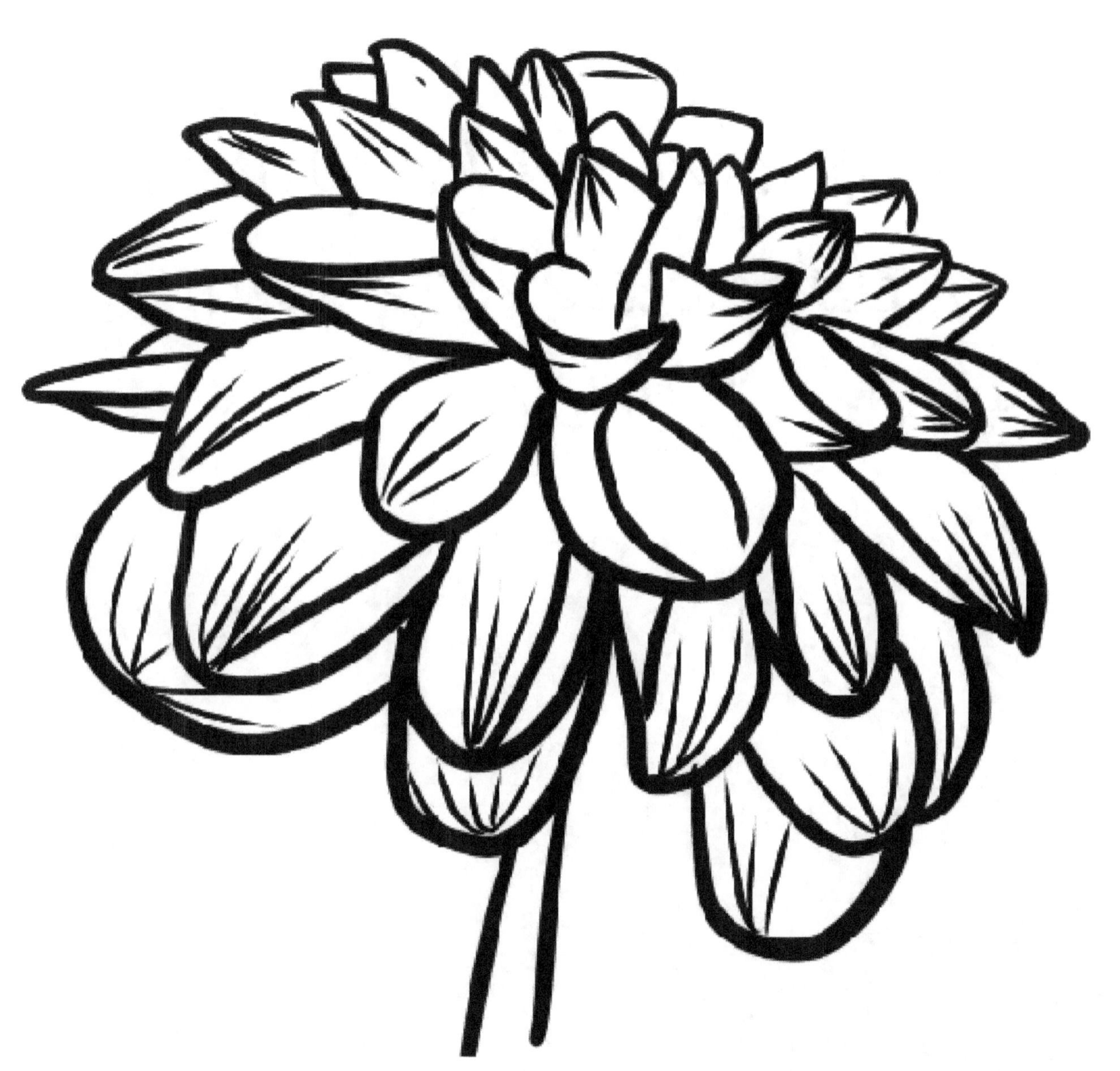

Nobody can keep you from achieving your goals.

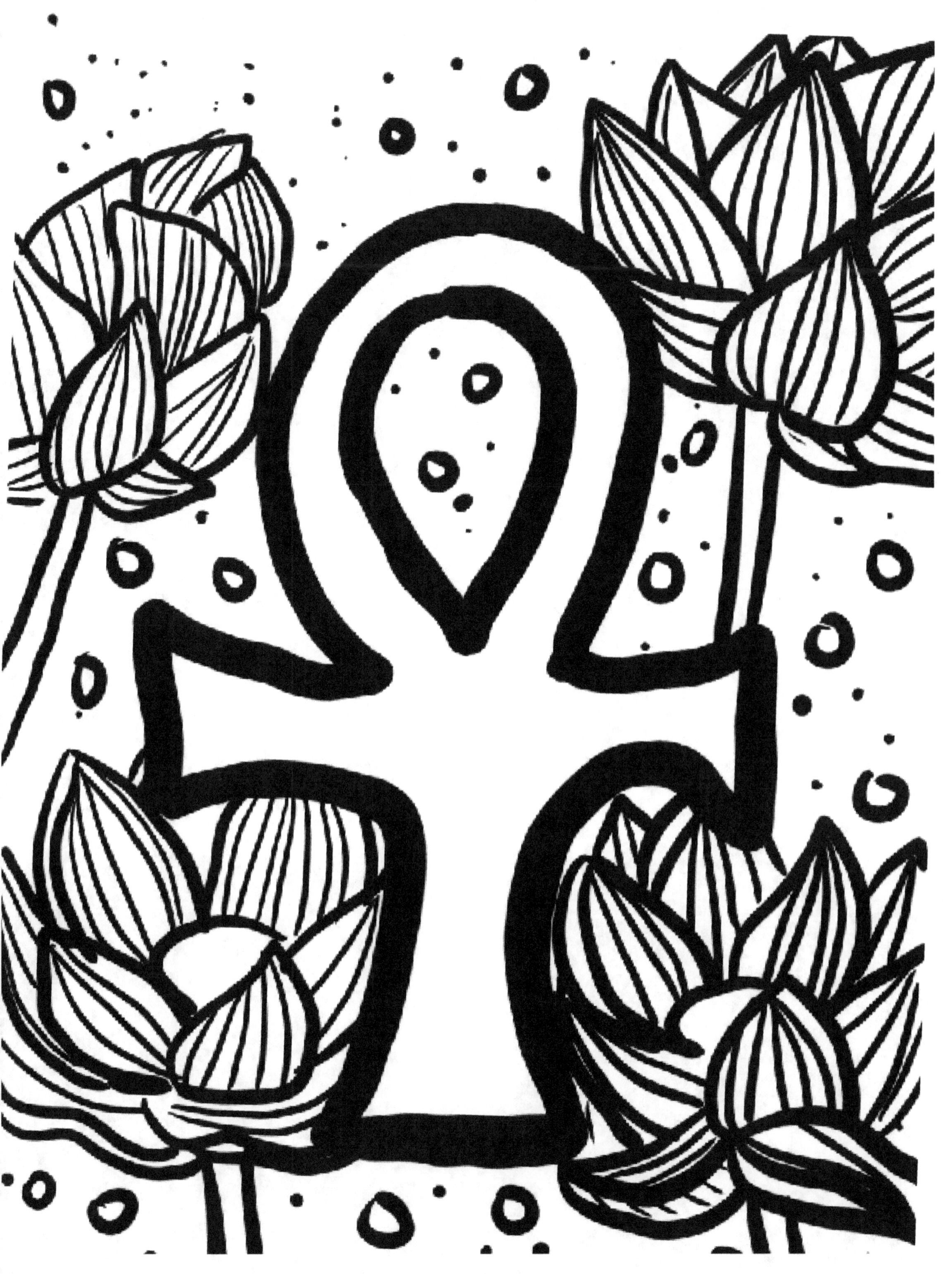

You are pretty enough.

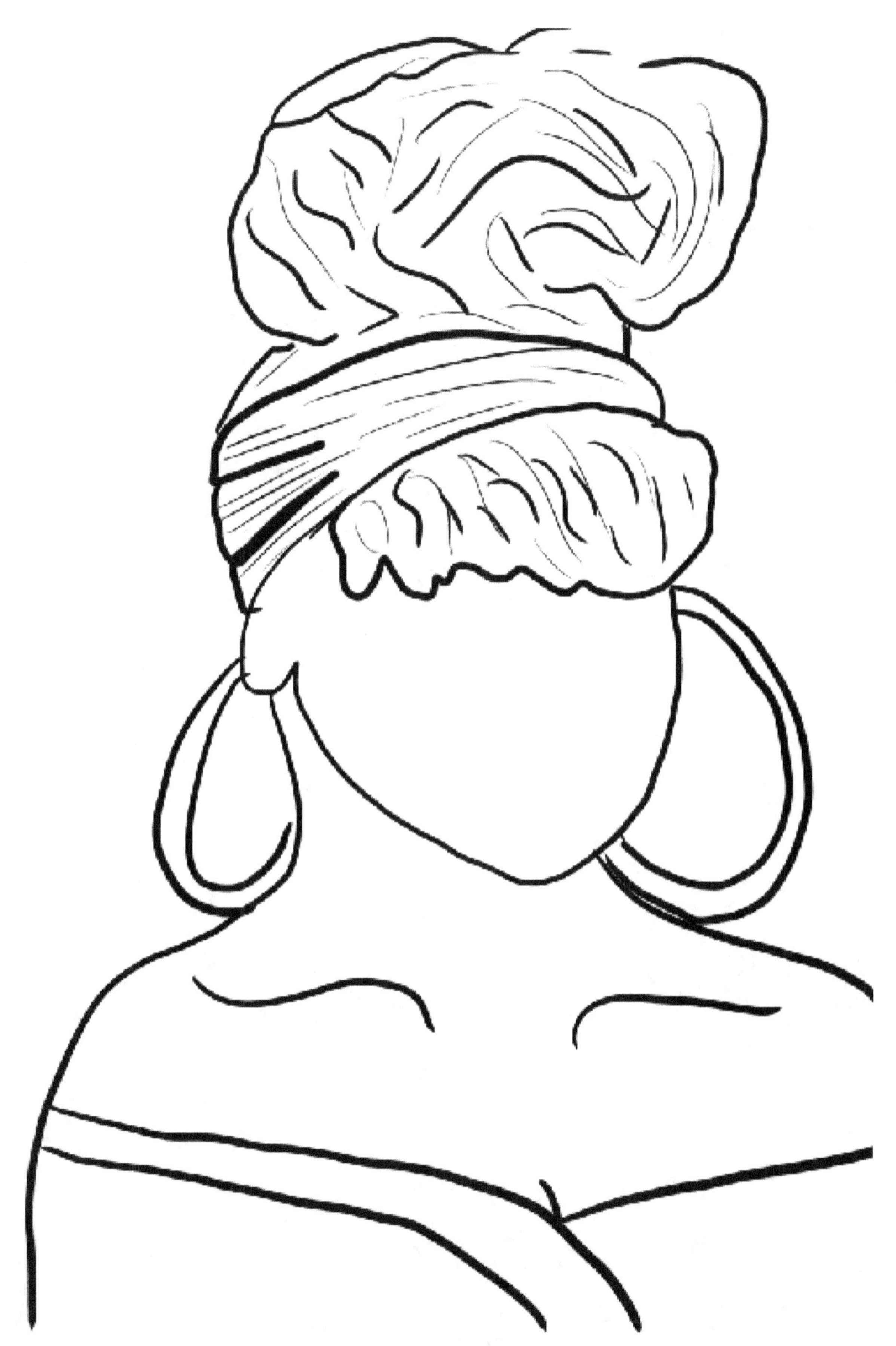

You deserve respect.

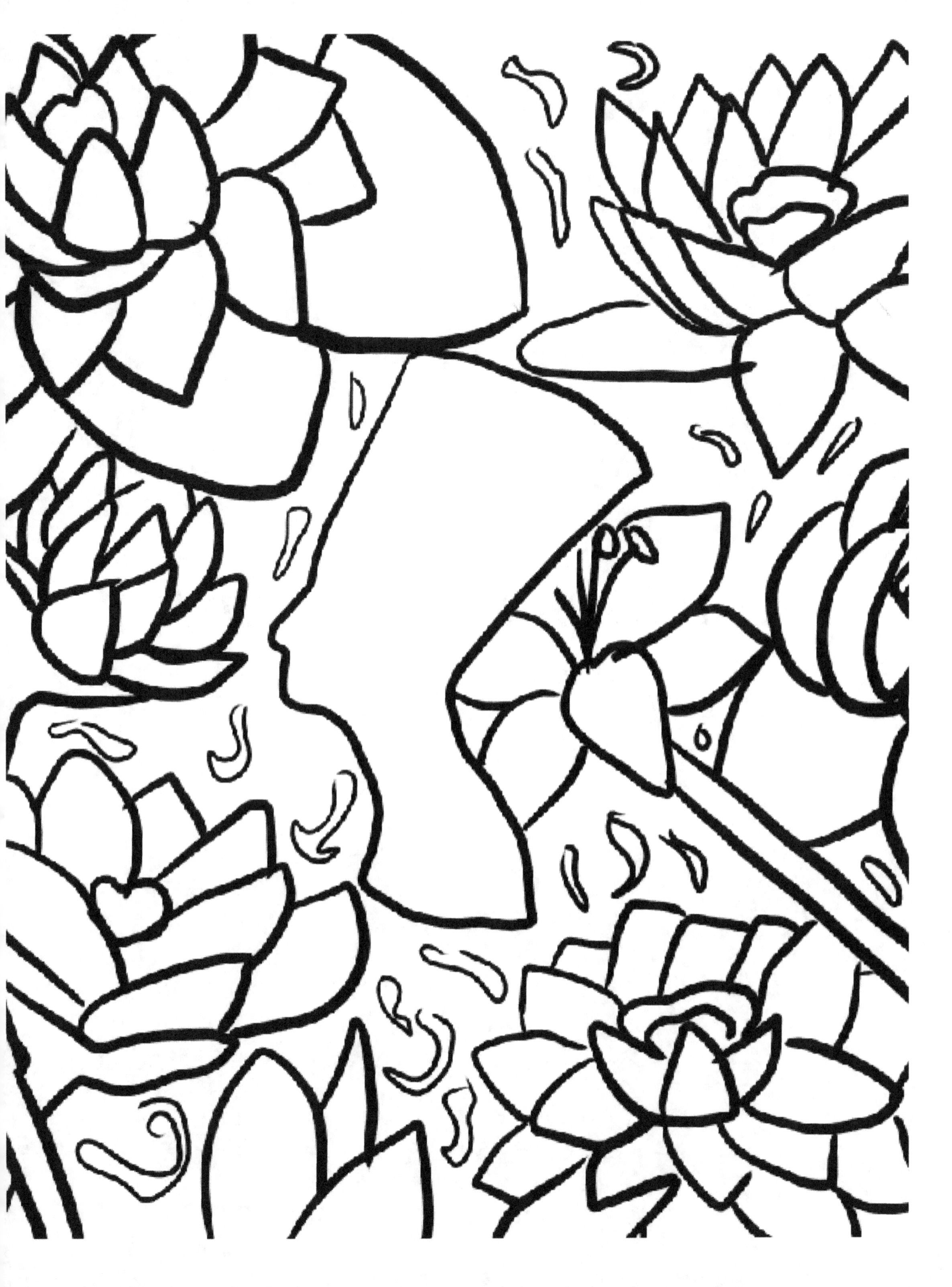

You aren't "too" dark.

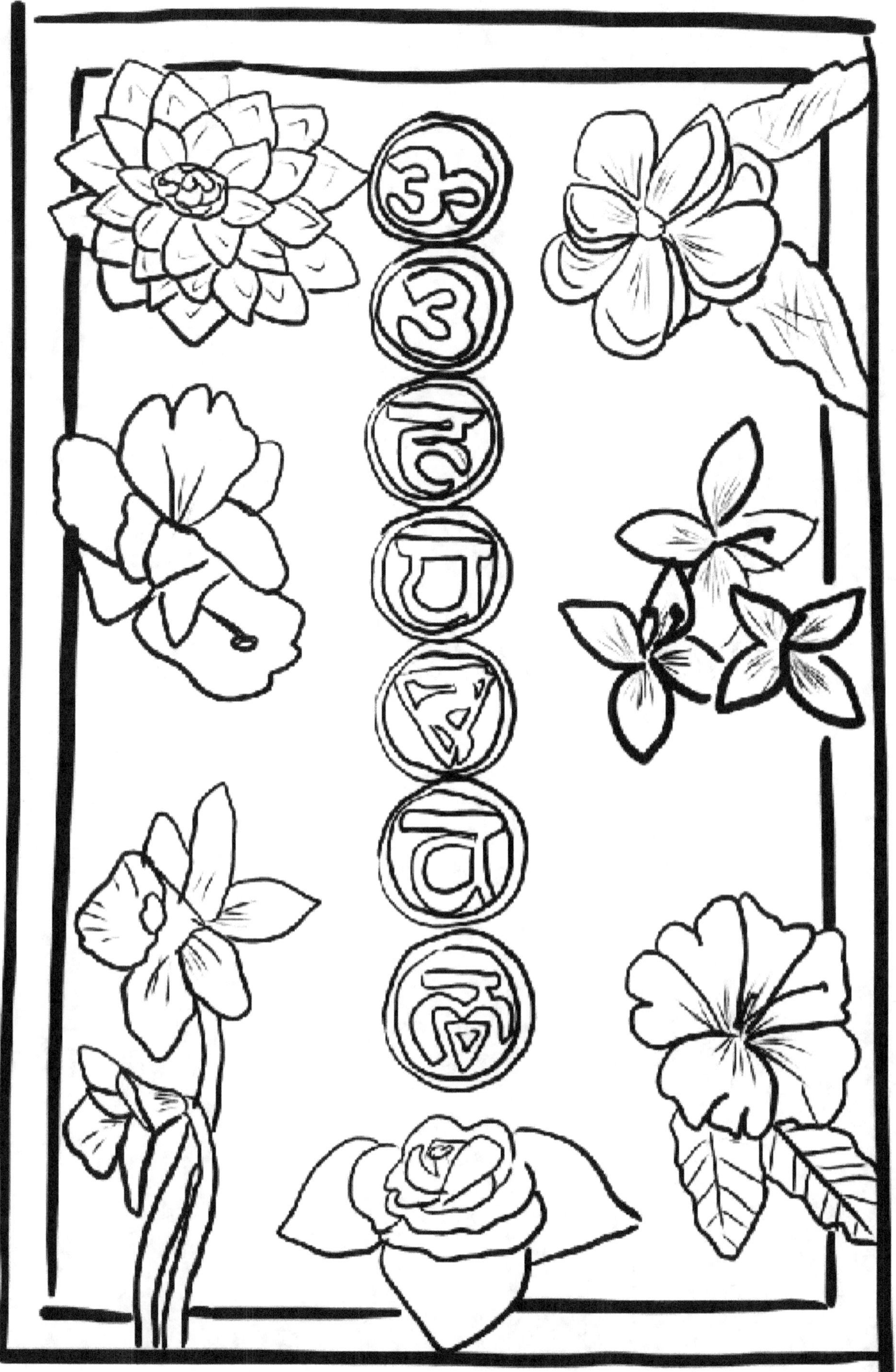

Love should not hurt.

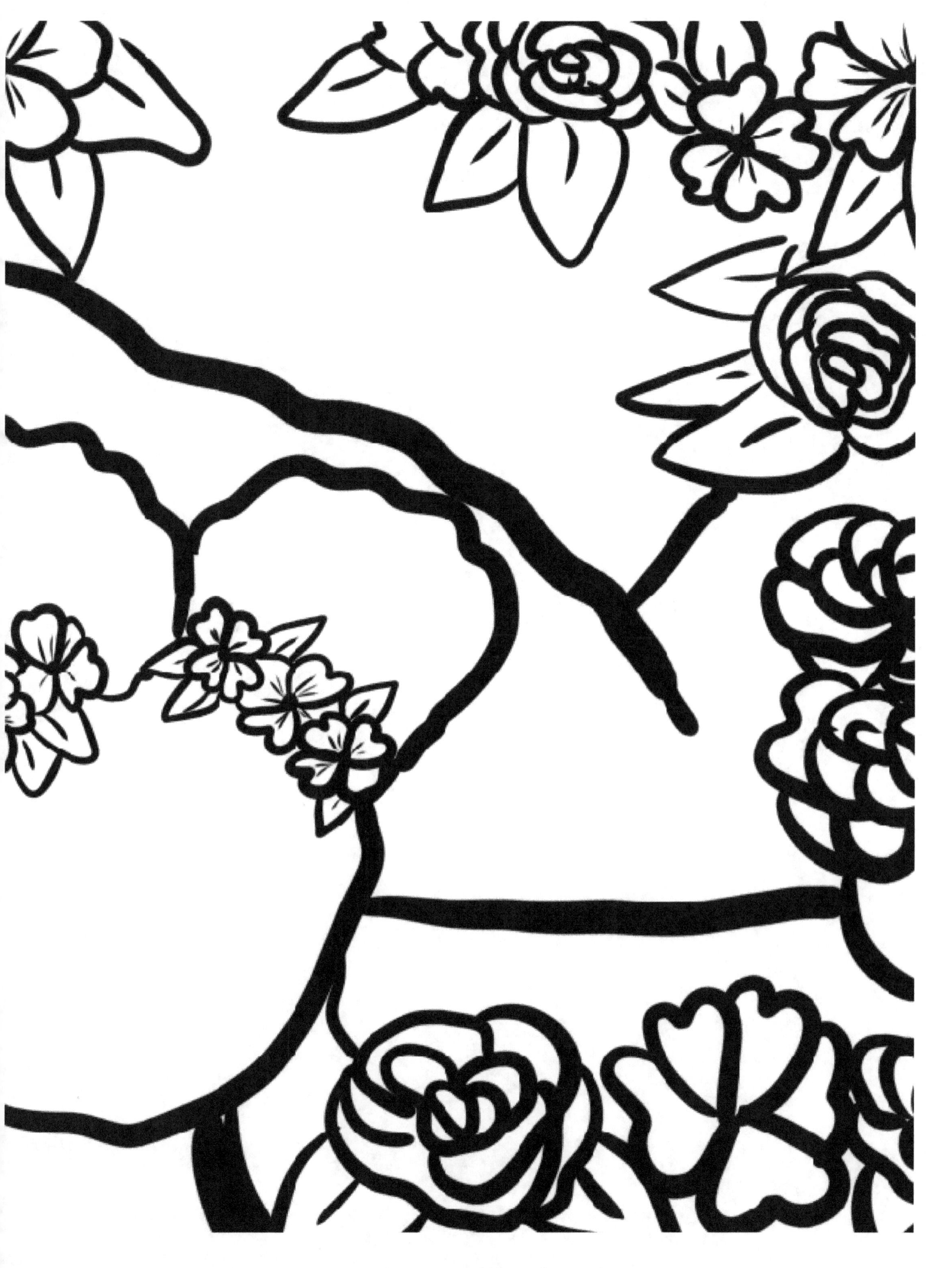

Your hair isn't nappy.

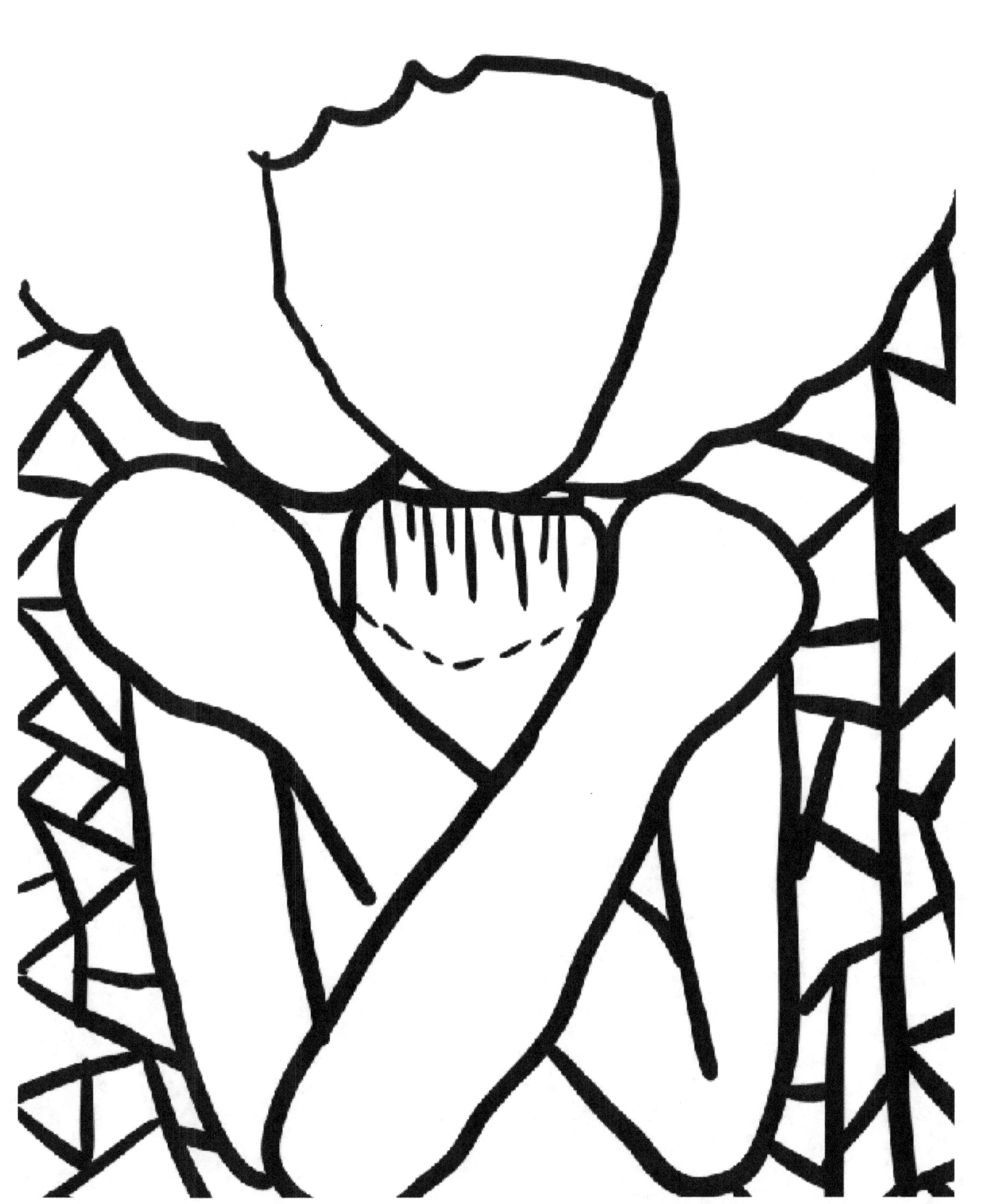

You deserve the world.

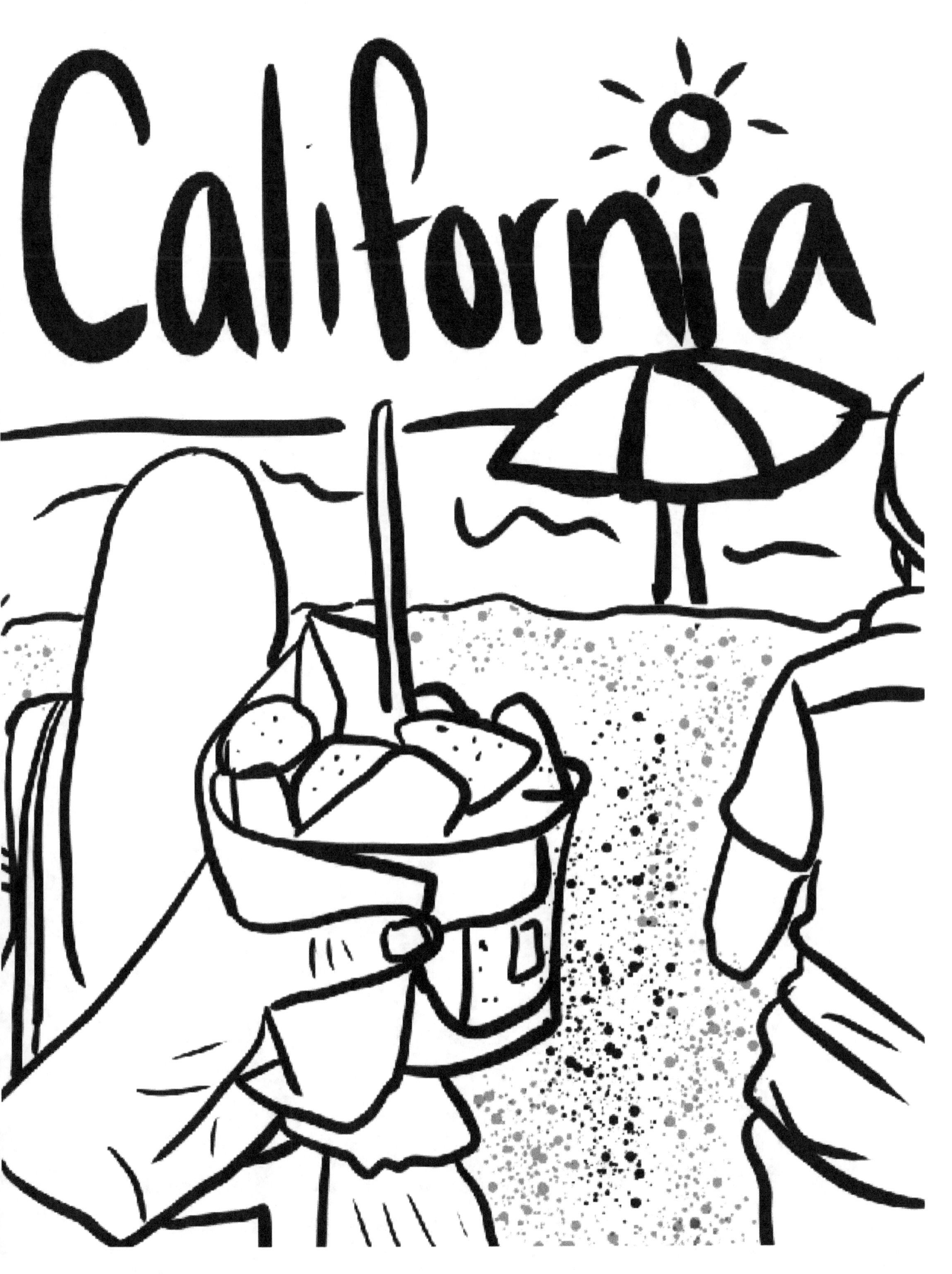
California

You deserve love.

LOVED

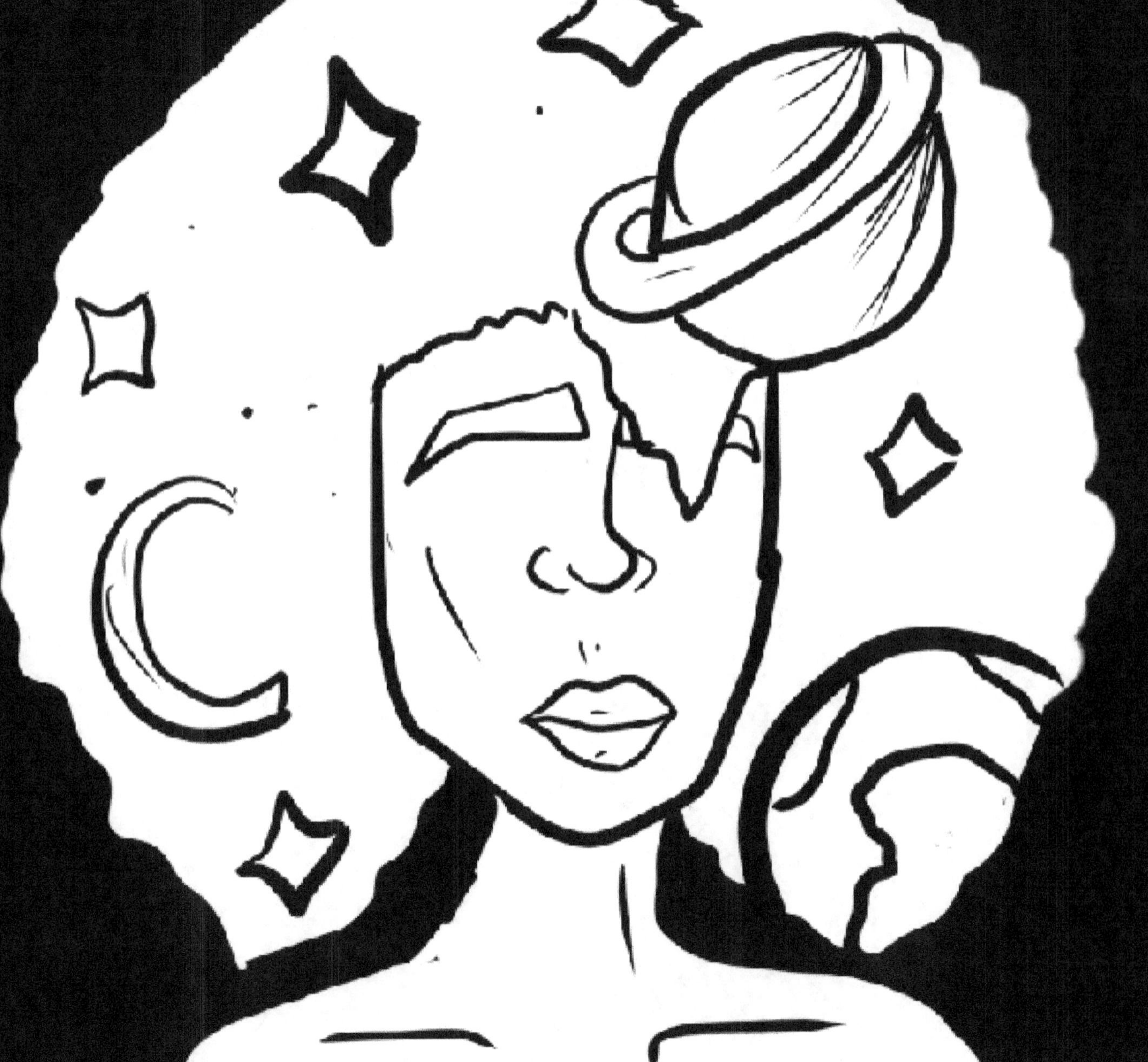

Nobody can stop a determined black woman.

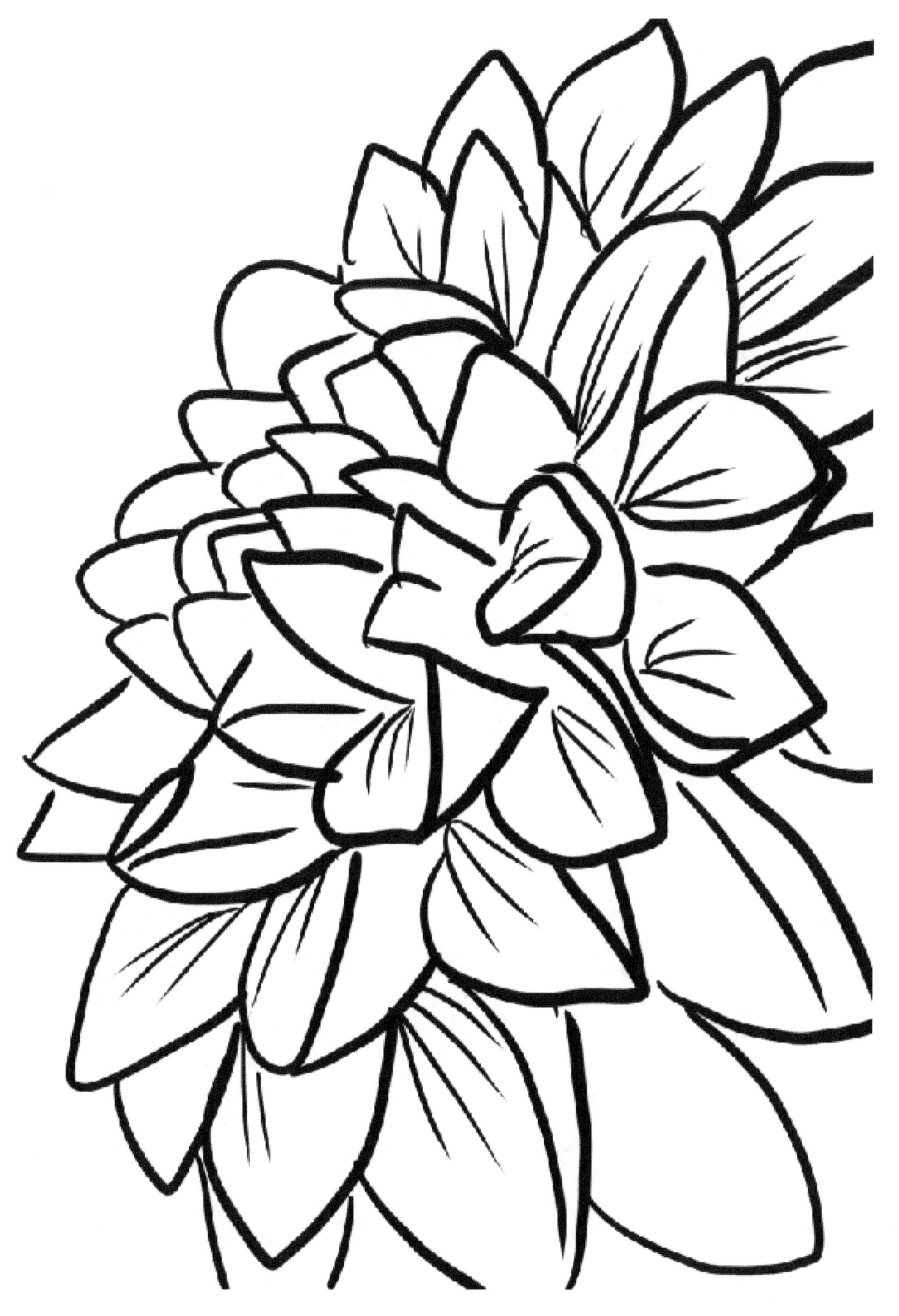

*Confidence breeds
beauty.*

You are unstoppable.

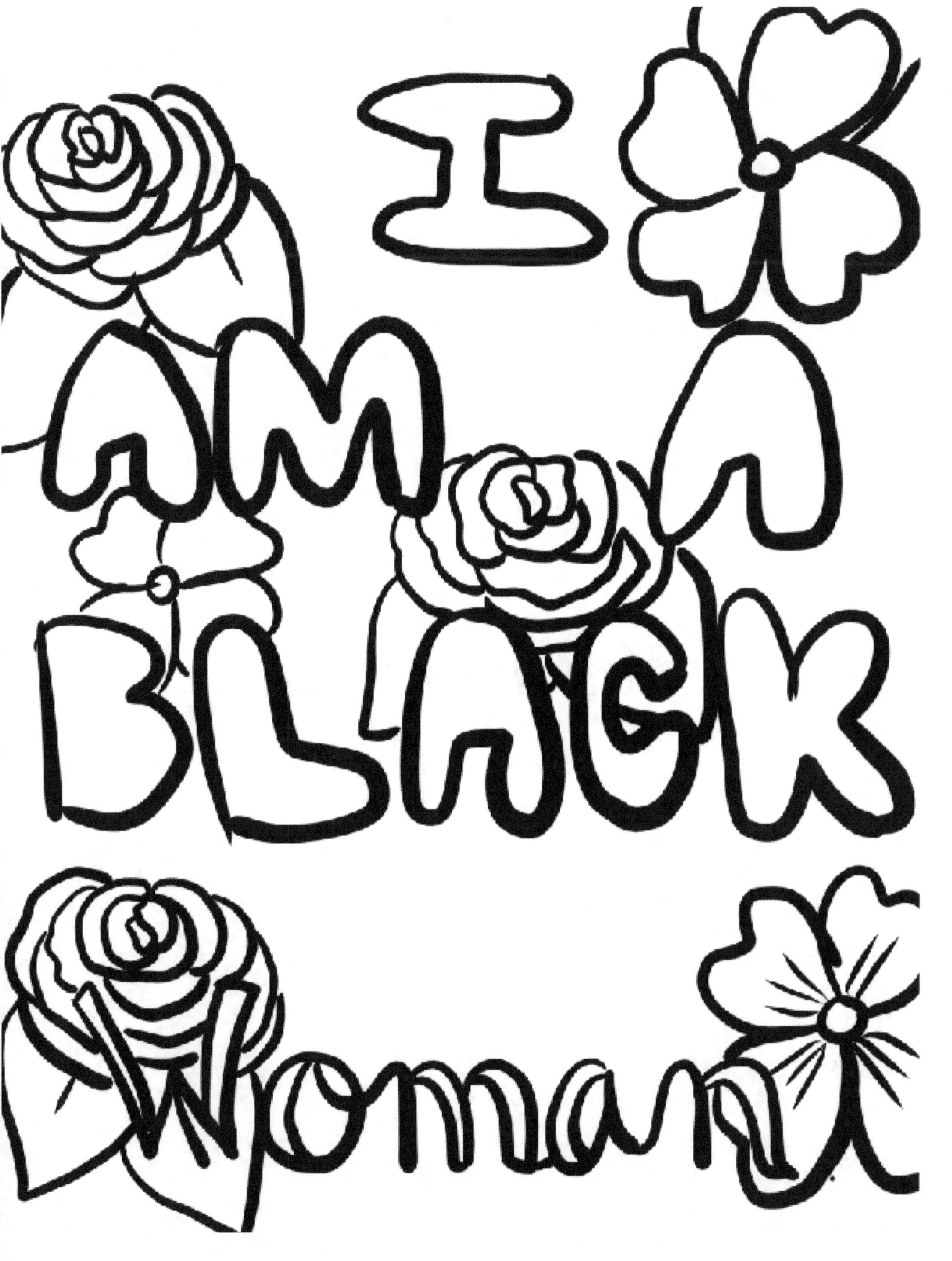

I
AM A
BLACK
Woman

You are loved.

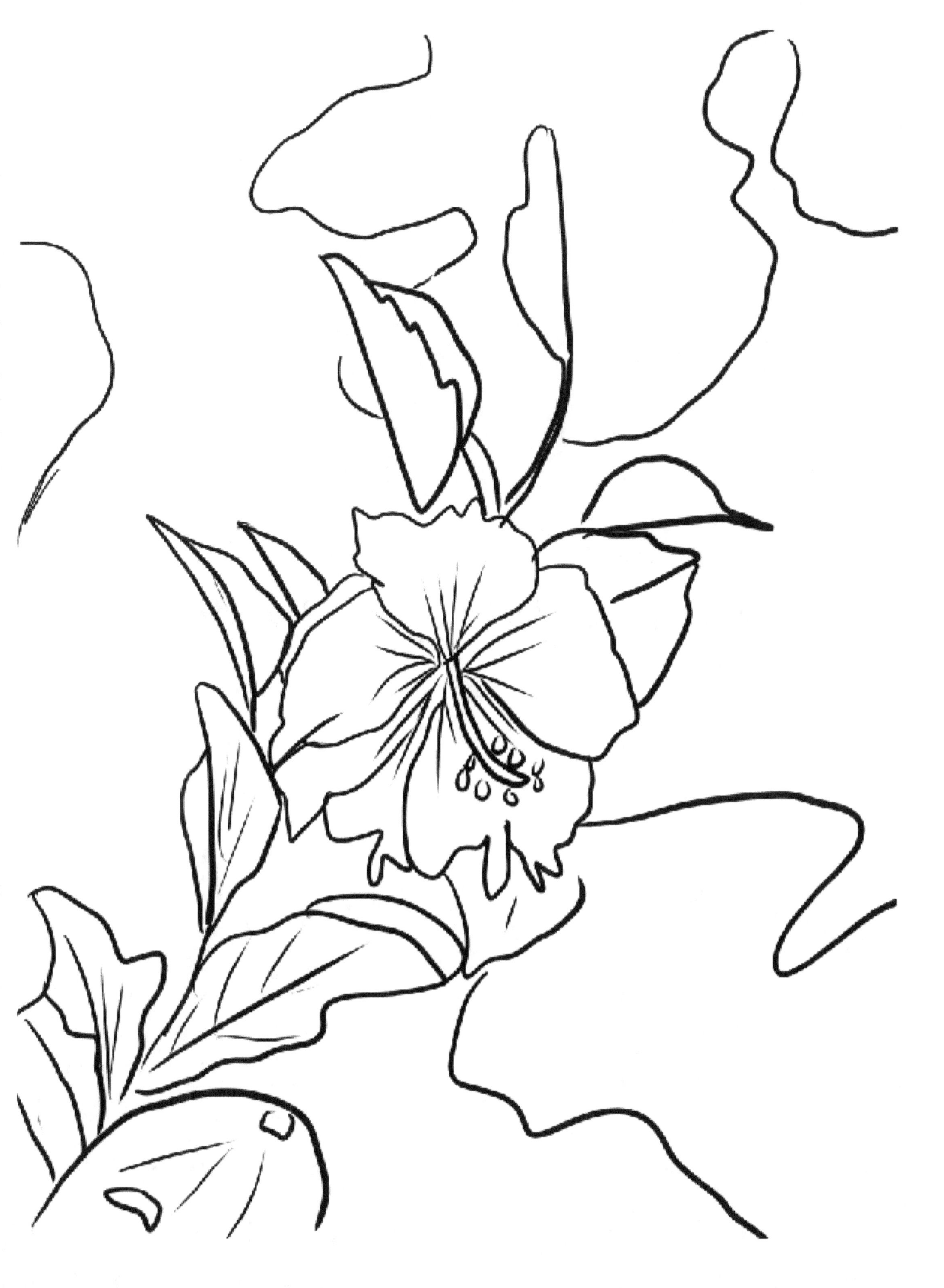

You are pretty enough.

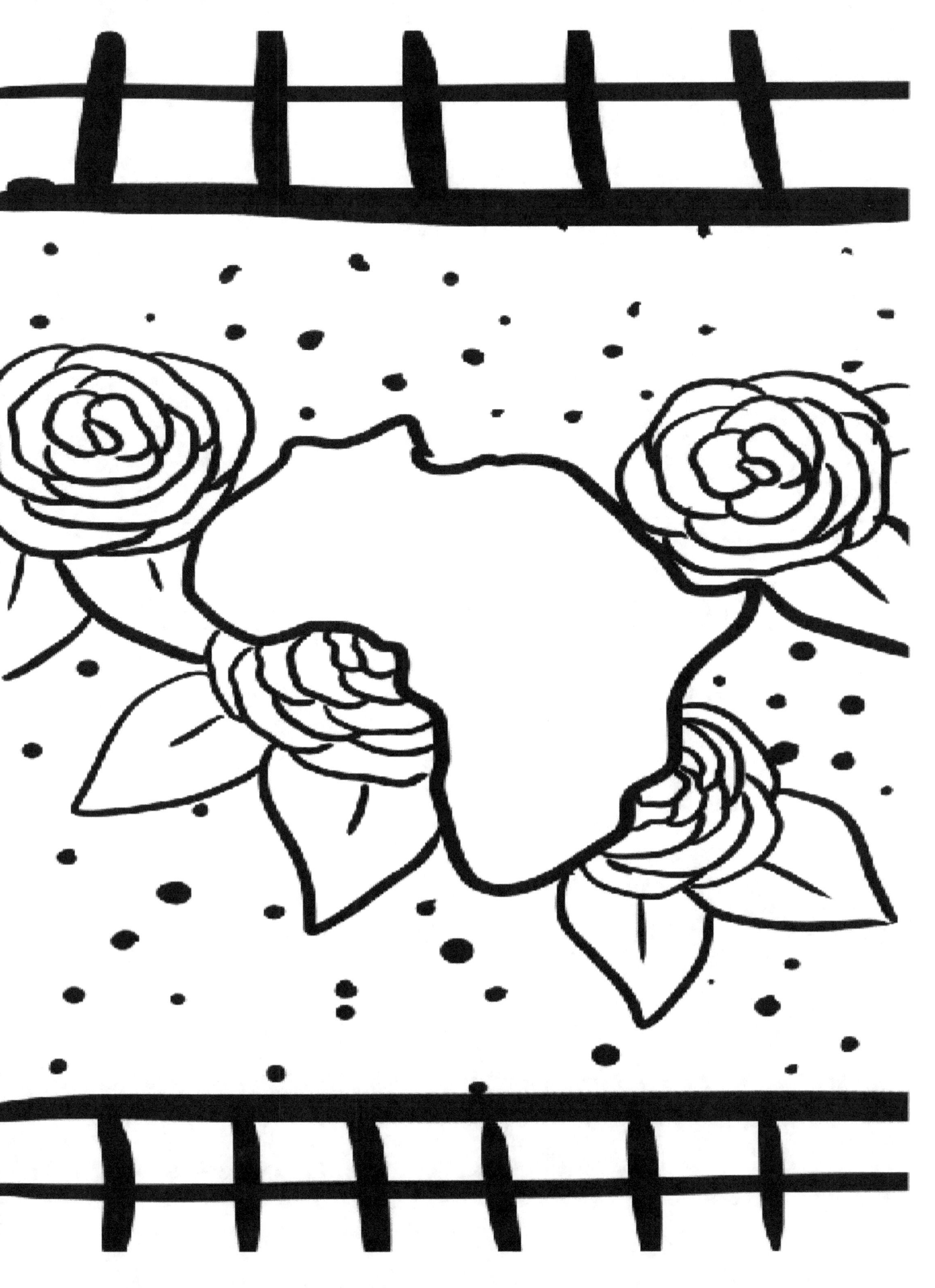

You deserve happiness.

You are important.

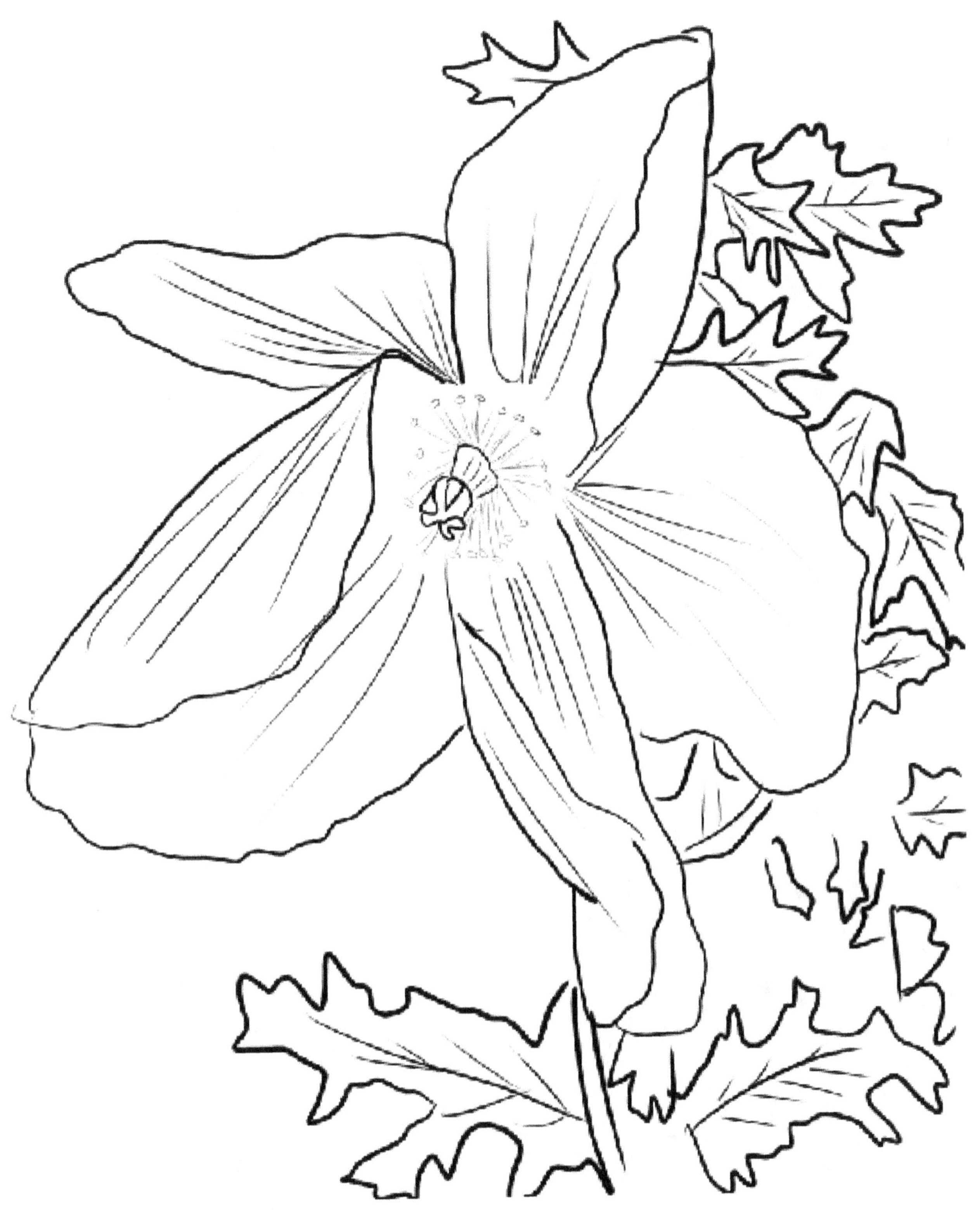

You are amazing.

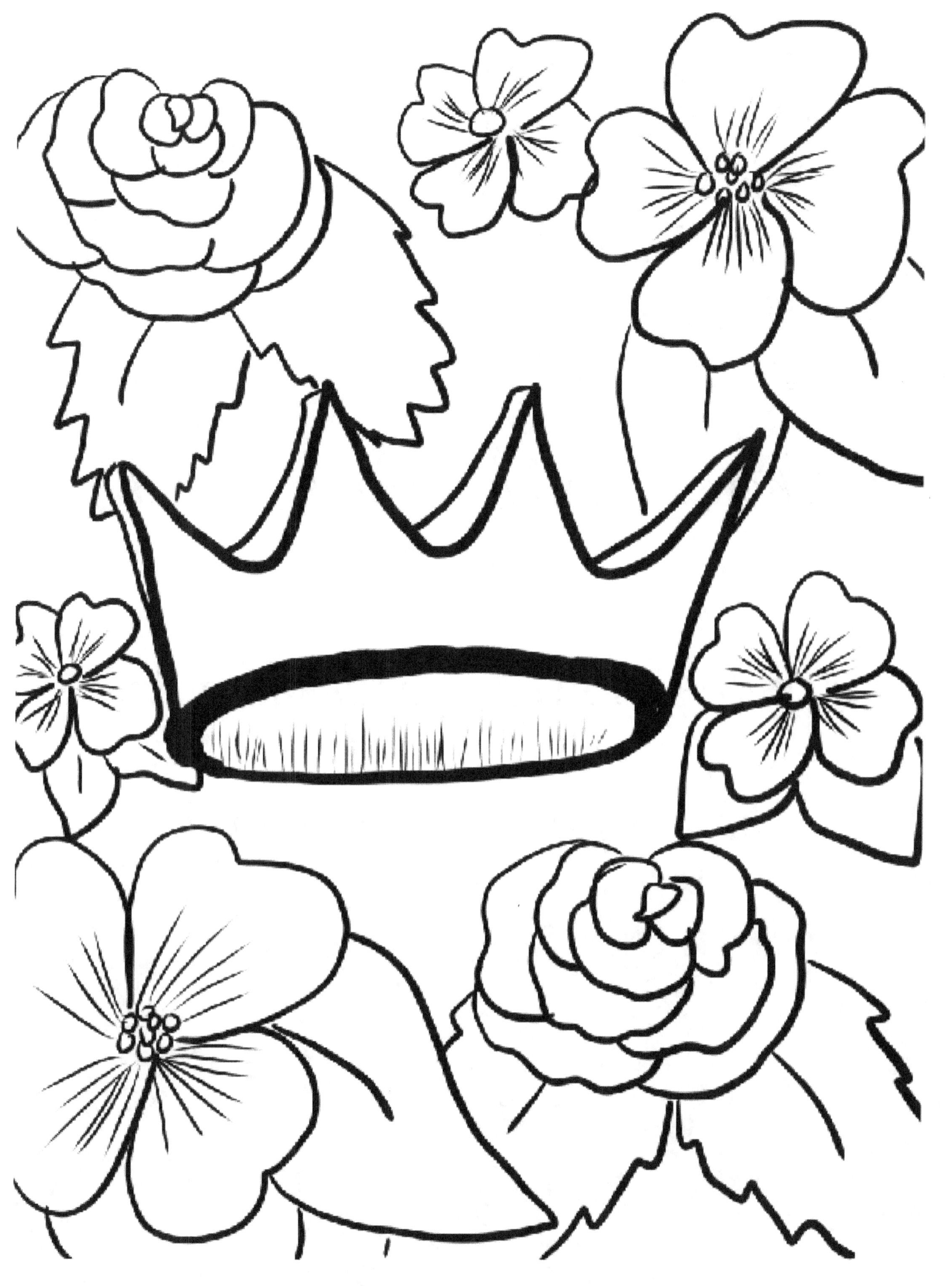

There is power in being a black
woman.

There is power in your melanin.

There is power in your smile.

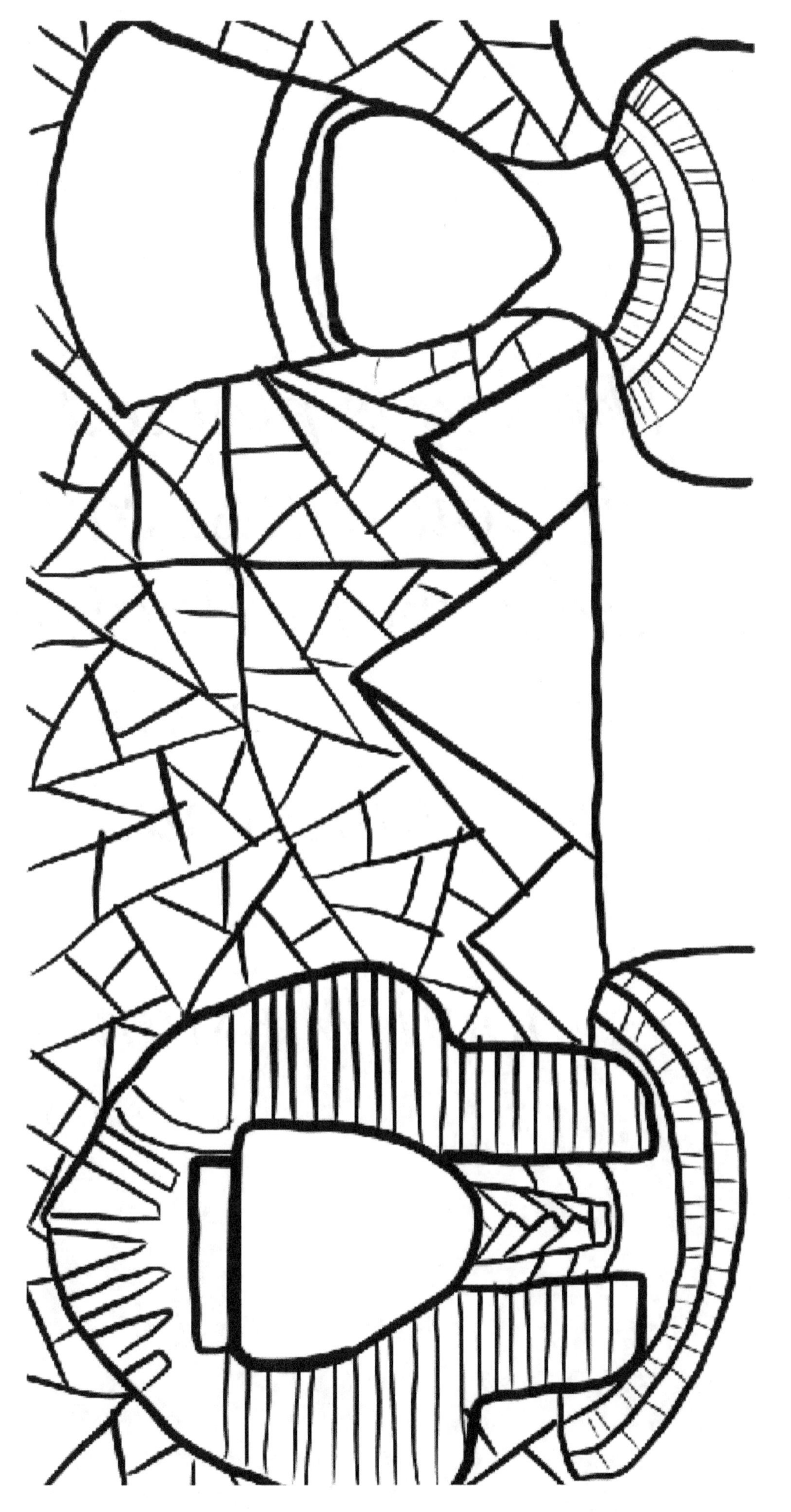

"The seeds planted within you will sprout the trees that will give shade to those who come behind you."

—Naomi Winston

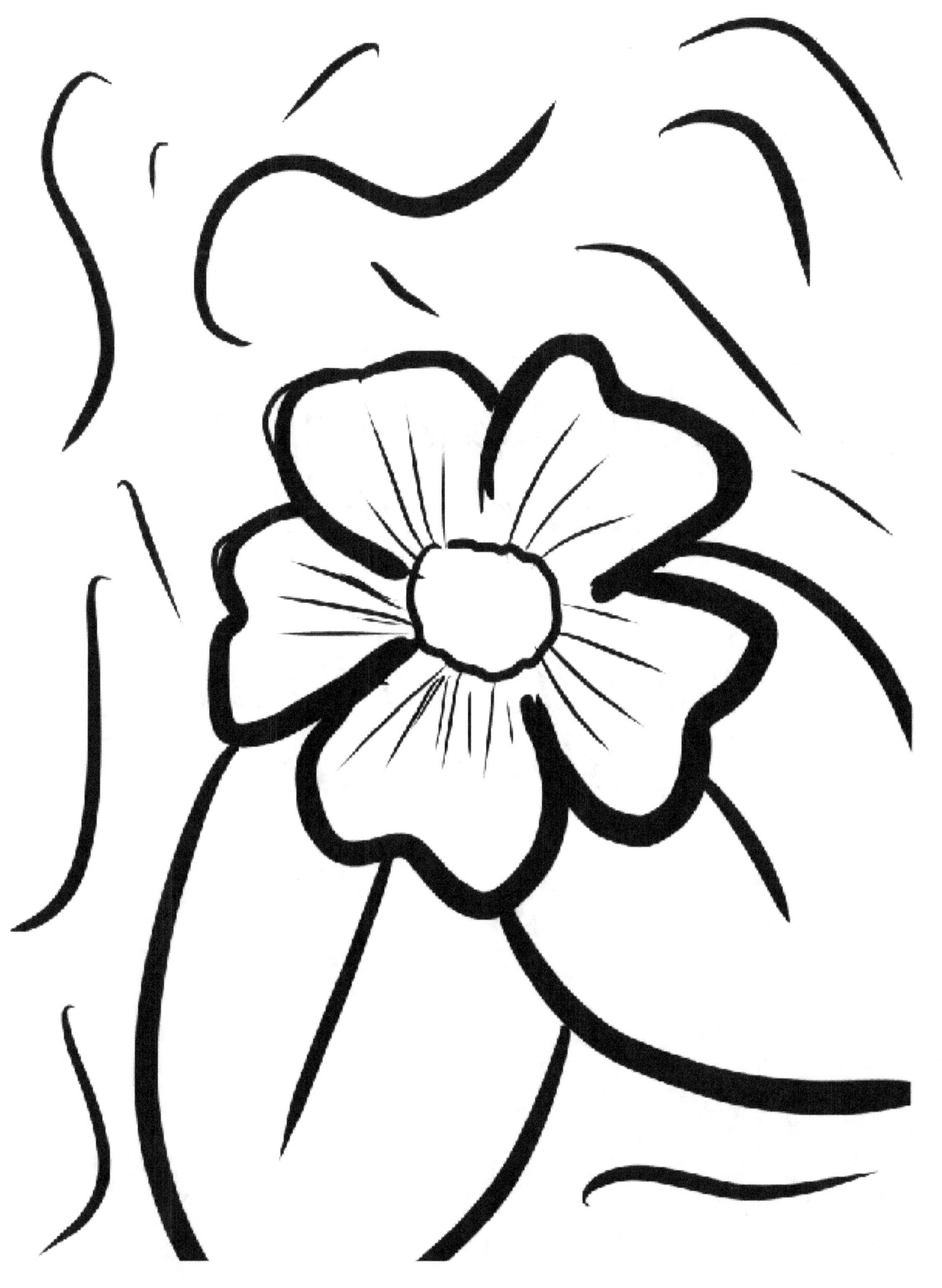

Your head scarf is
your crown.

Wear it proudly and
without shame.

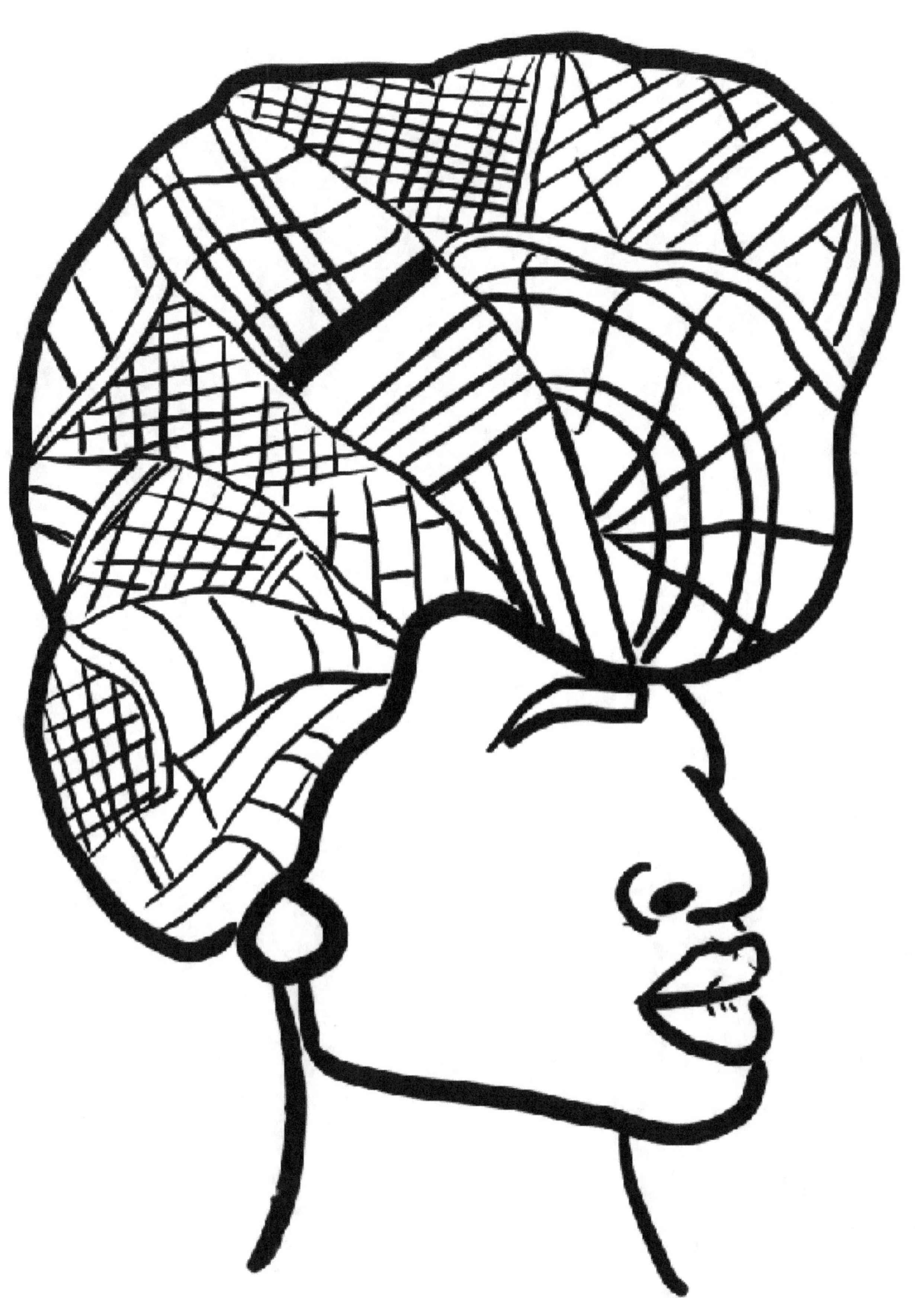

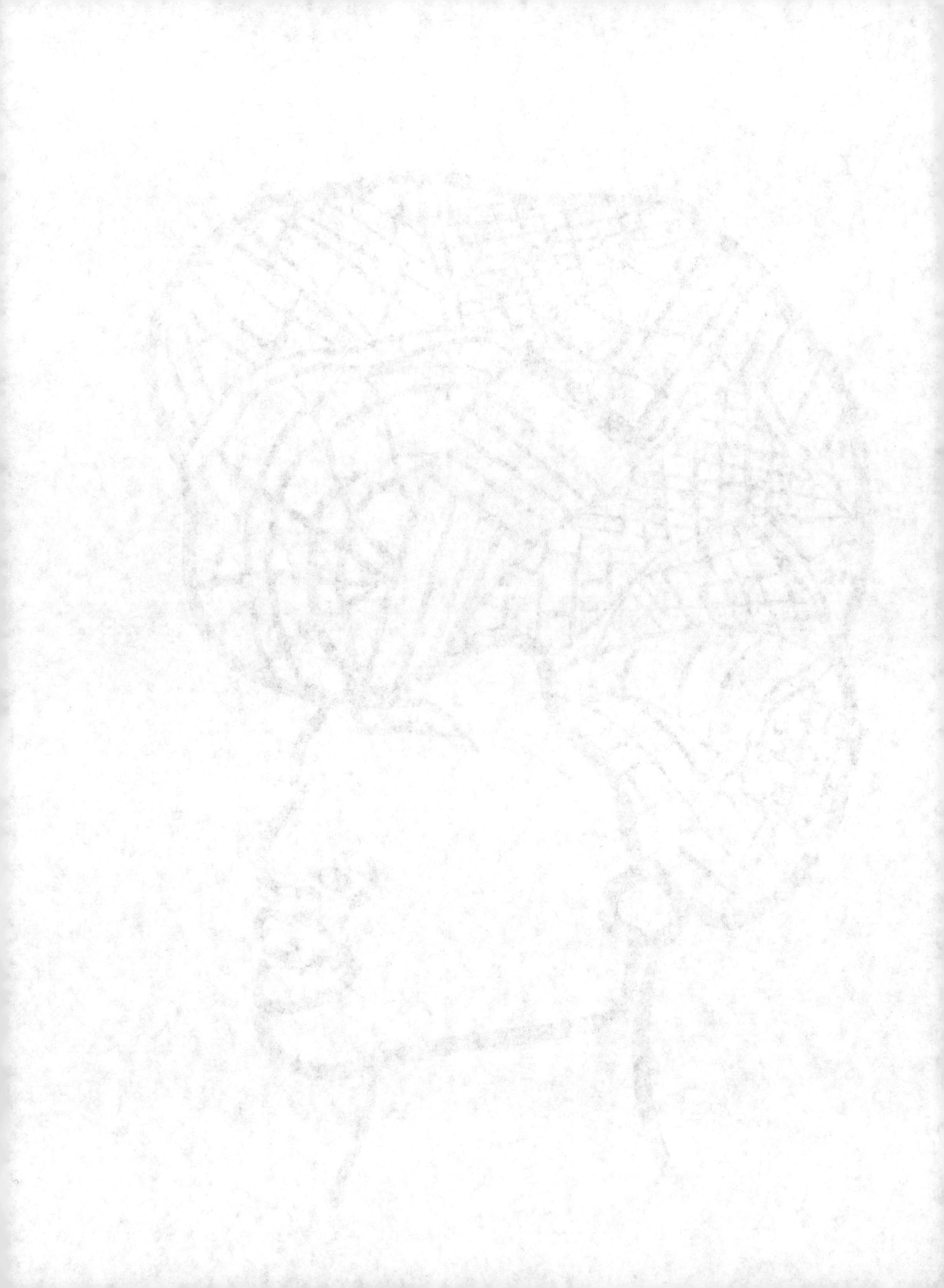

Those who have done it before...

This category is full of black women in history and presently who have taken significant strides in their areas. Because of these women doors have been opened for us that would otherwise be closed. They opened the door for us to prove that we can do it and so we can do it for others. If you don't believe in yourself know that these women sacrificed so you could have a chance.

"A racist system inevitably destroys and hurts human beings; it brutalizes and dehumanizes them, black and whites alike."

—Mamie Phipps Clark (American psychologist)

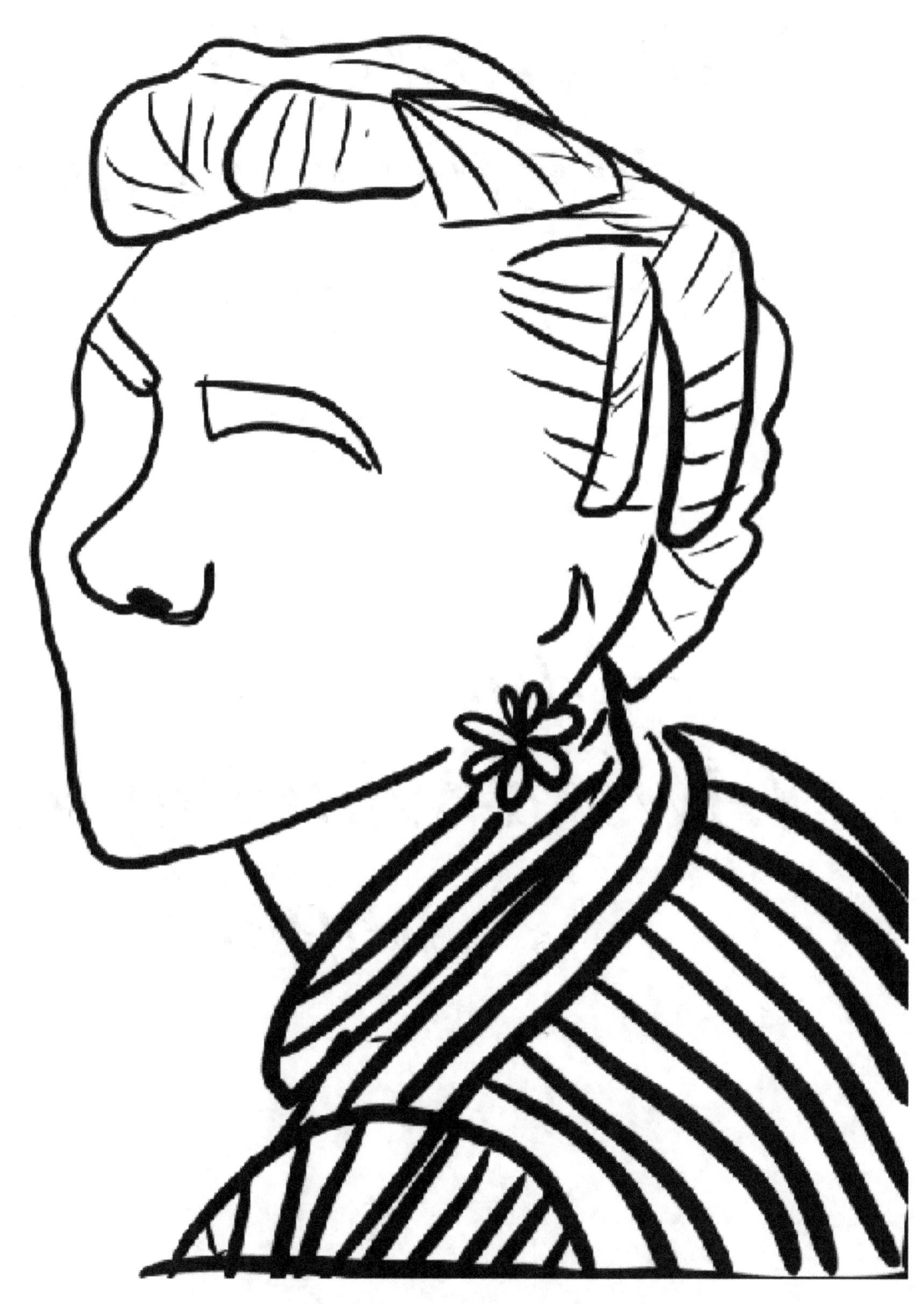

" *Blues are the songs of despair but gospel songs are the songs of hope.*"

—*Mahalia Jackson (Award-winning gospel singer)*

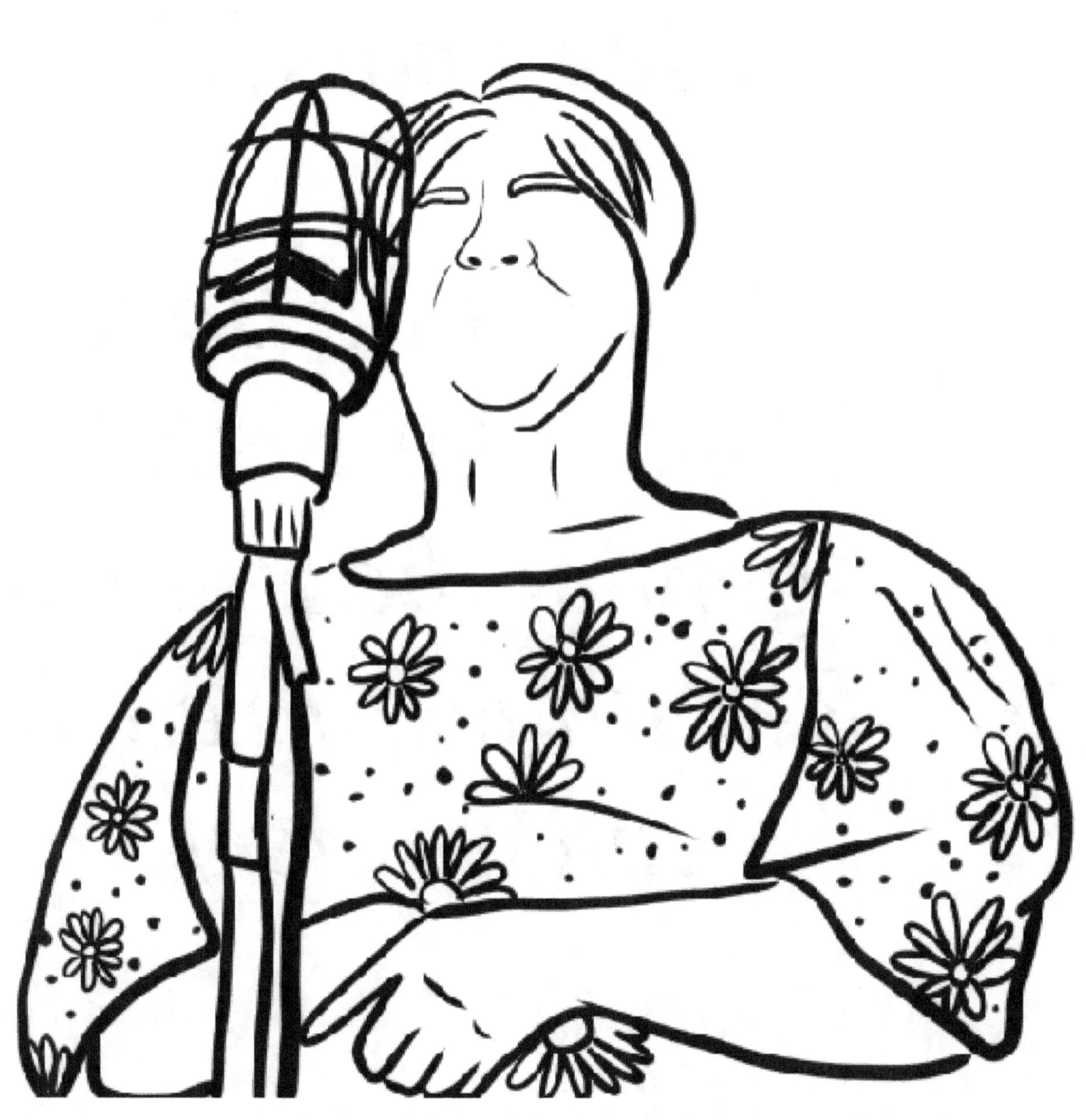

"The things we truly love stay with us, locked in our hearts as long as life remains."

—Josephine Baker (civil rights activist/ Agent of the French Resistance/ French entertainer)

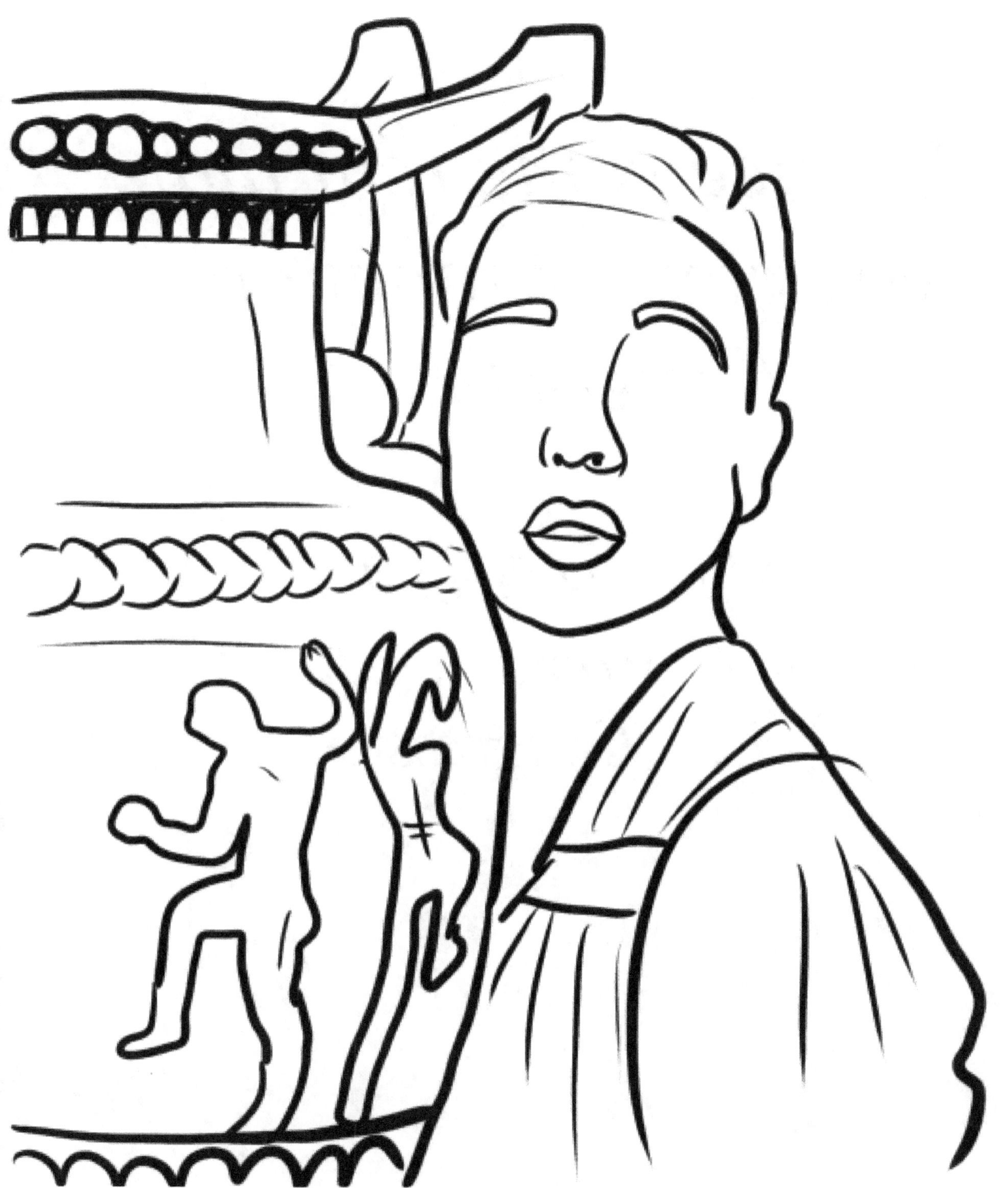

"Service is the rent that you pay for room on this earth."

—Shirley Chisholm
First black woman elected to U.S. Congress

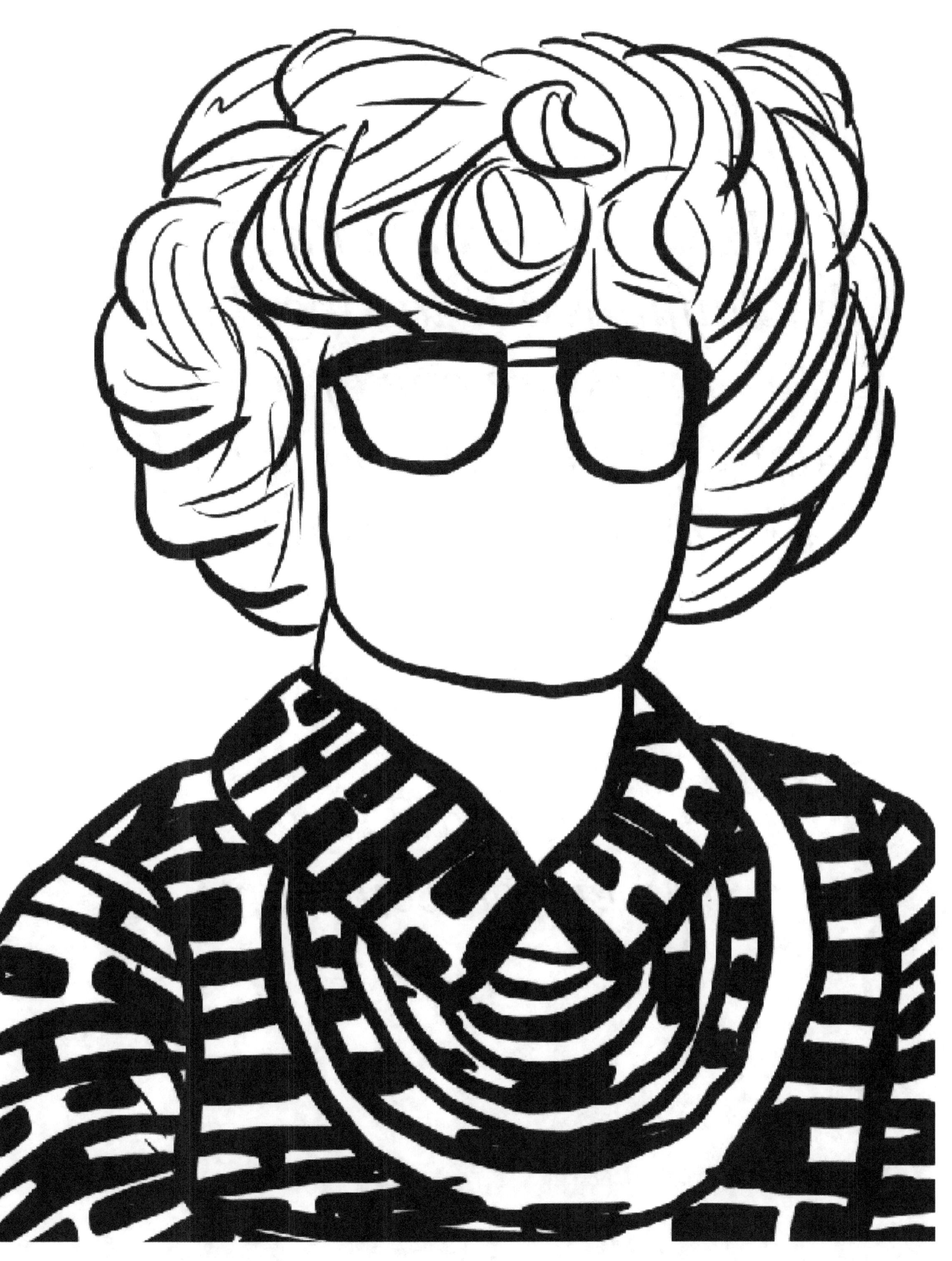

"I have created nothing really beautiful, really lasting, but if I can inspire one of these youngsters to develop the talent I know they possess, then my monument will be in their work."

—Augusta Savage
(American Sculptor)

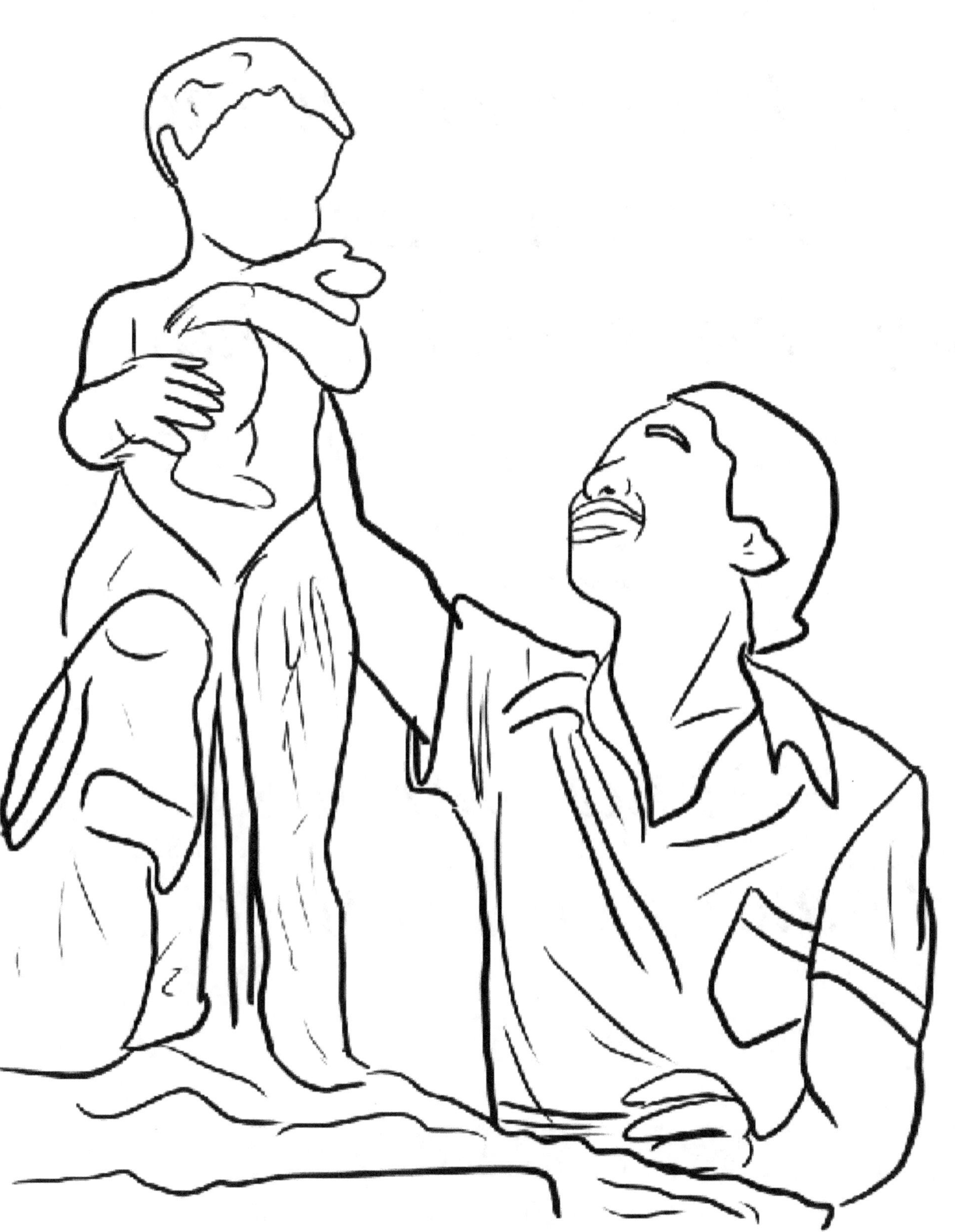

"Through color I have sought to concentrate on beauty and happiness, rather than on man's inhumanity to man."

—*Alma Thomas*
(American Painter)

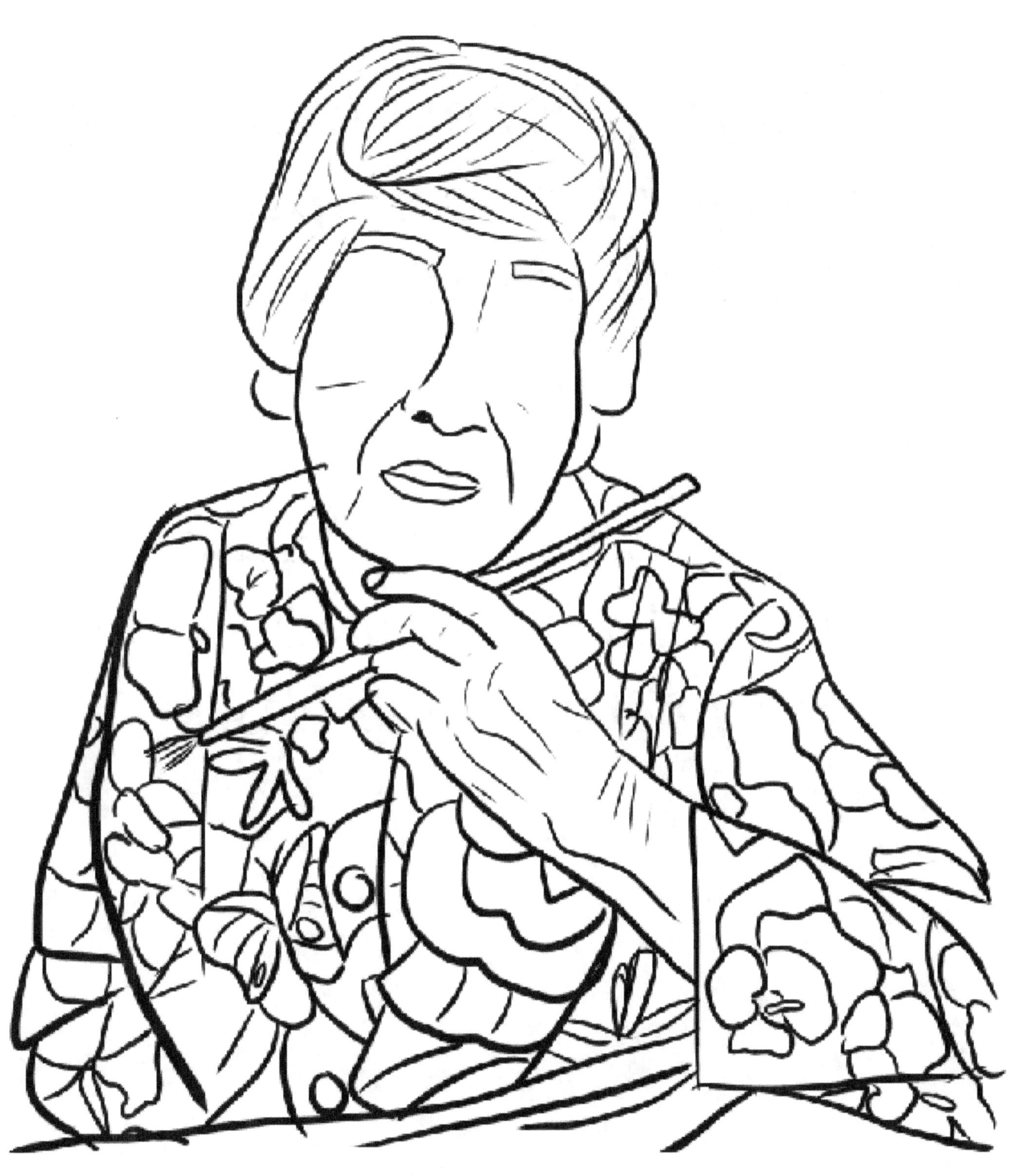

"I knew well that the only way I could get the door open was to knock it down; because I knocked all of them down."

—Charlotte E. Ray
(First black woman become a lawyer in the U.S.)

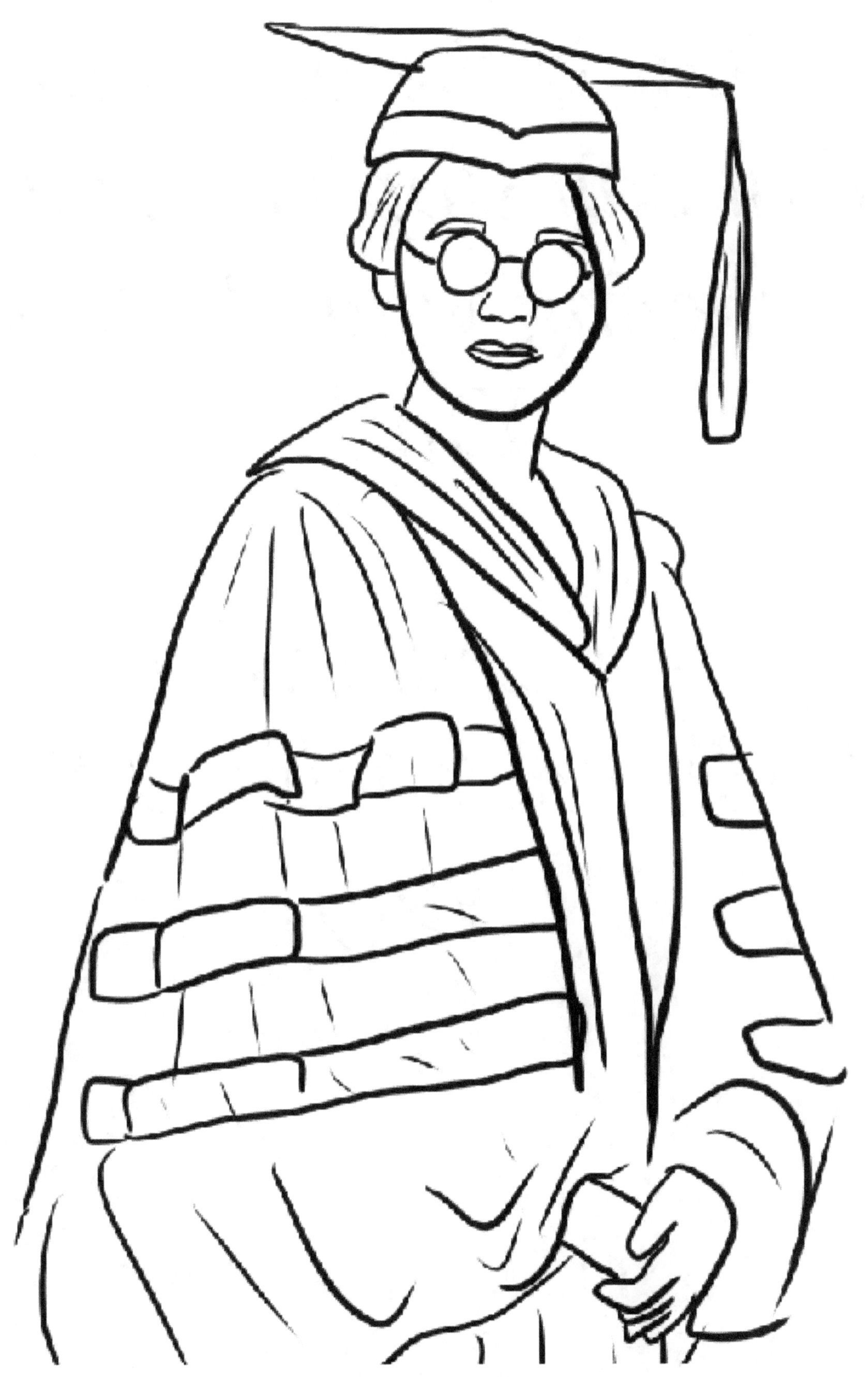

"What is the only thing that can stop you from achieving your destiny? You."

—Carole Gist (First black Miss U.S.A. 1990)

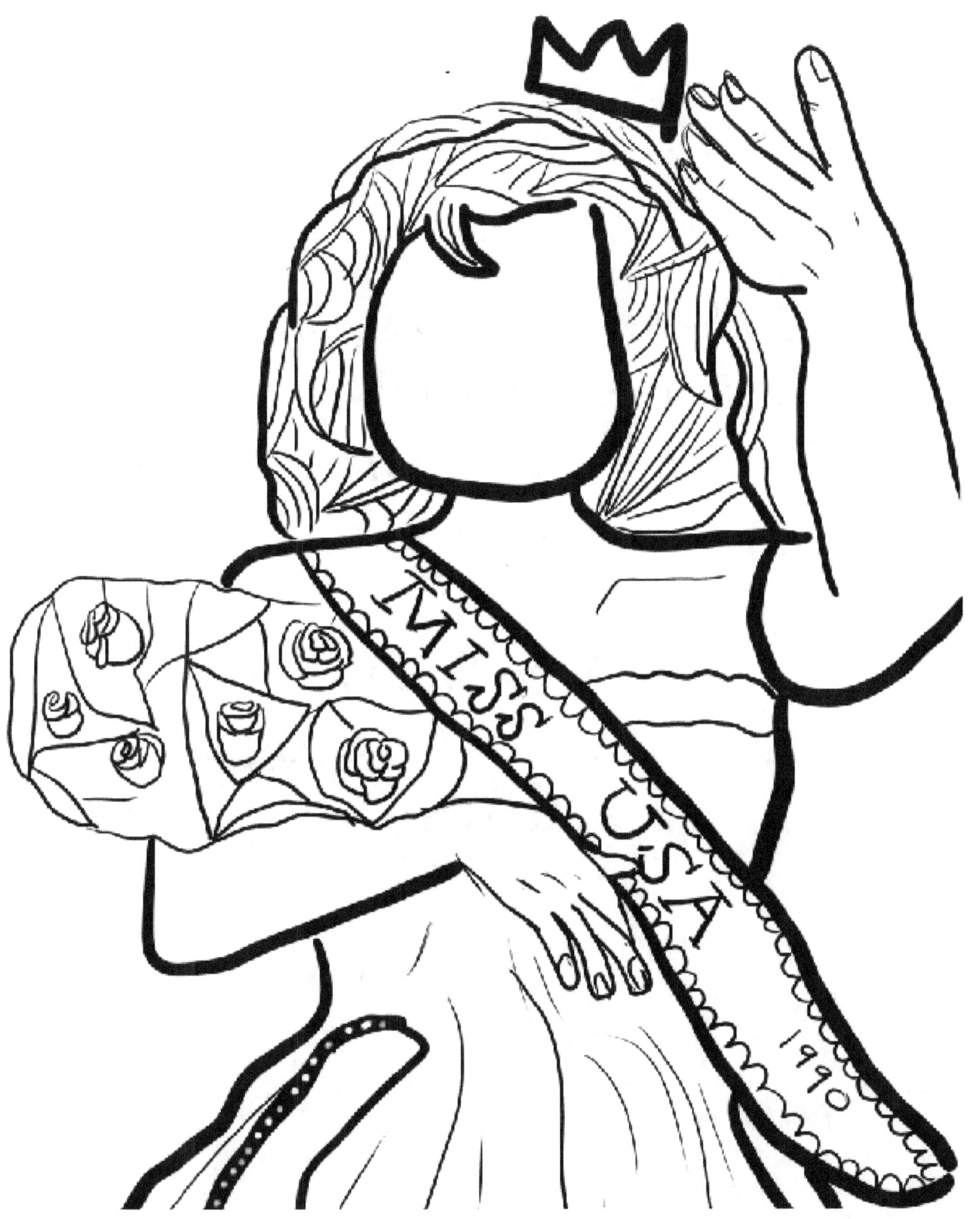
MISS USA
1990

"There's no excuse for the young people not knowing who the heroes and heroines are or were."

—Nina Simone
Musical Artist/Civil Rights Activist

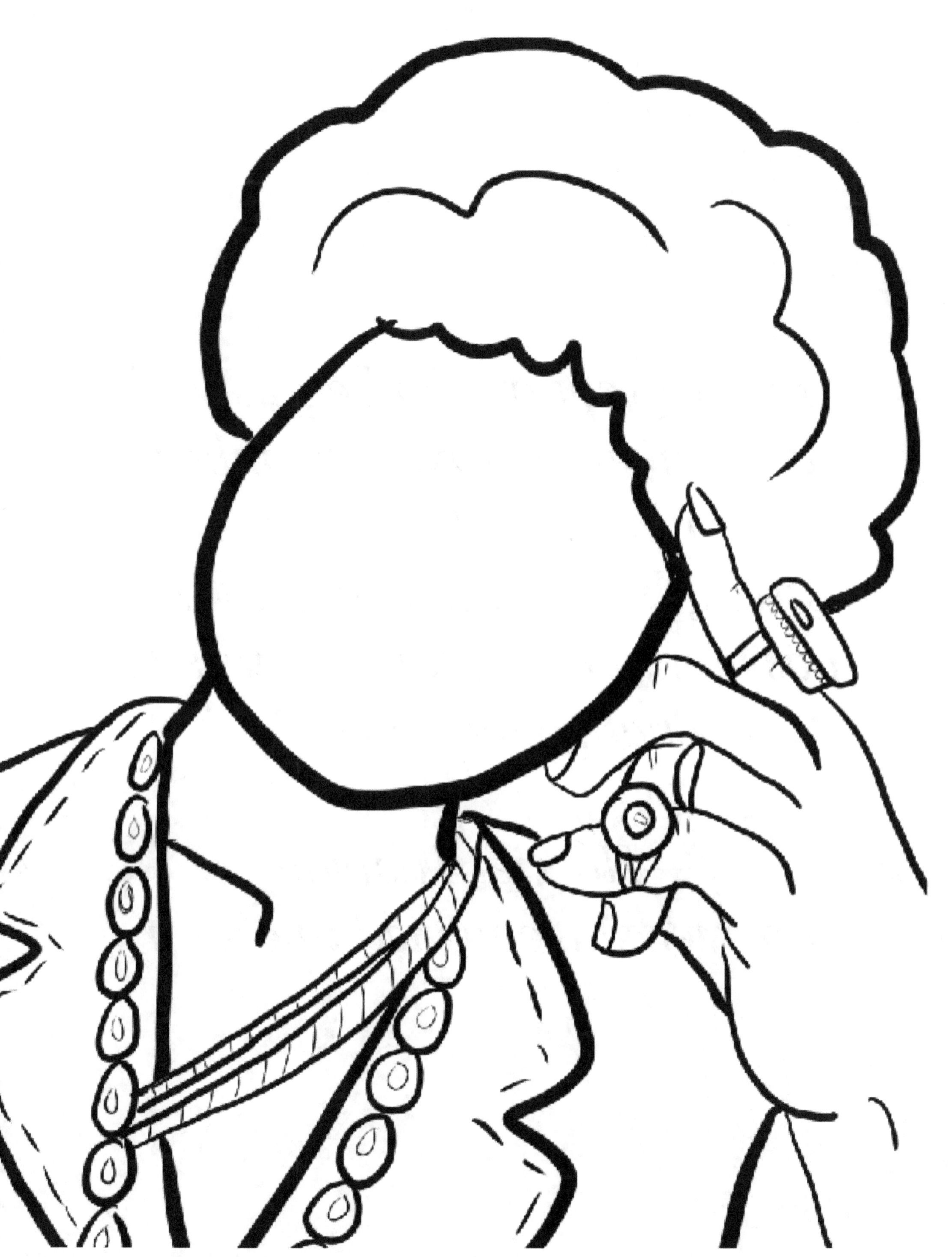

"Every great dream begins with a dreamer. Always remember, you have within you the strength, the patience, and the passion to reach for the stars to change the world."

—Harriet Tubman
Former slave turned liberator

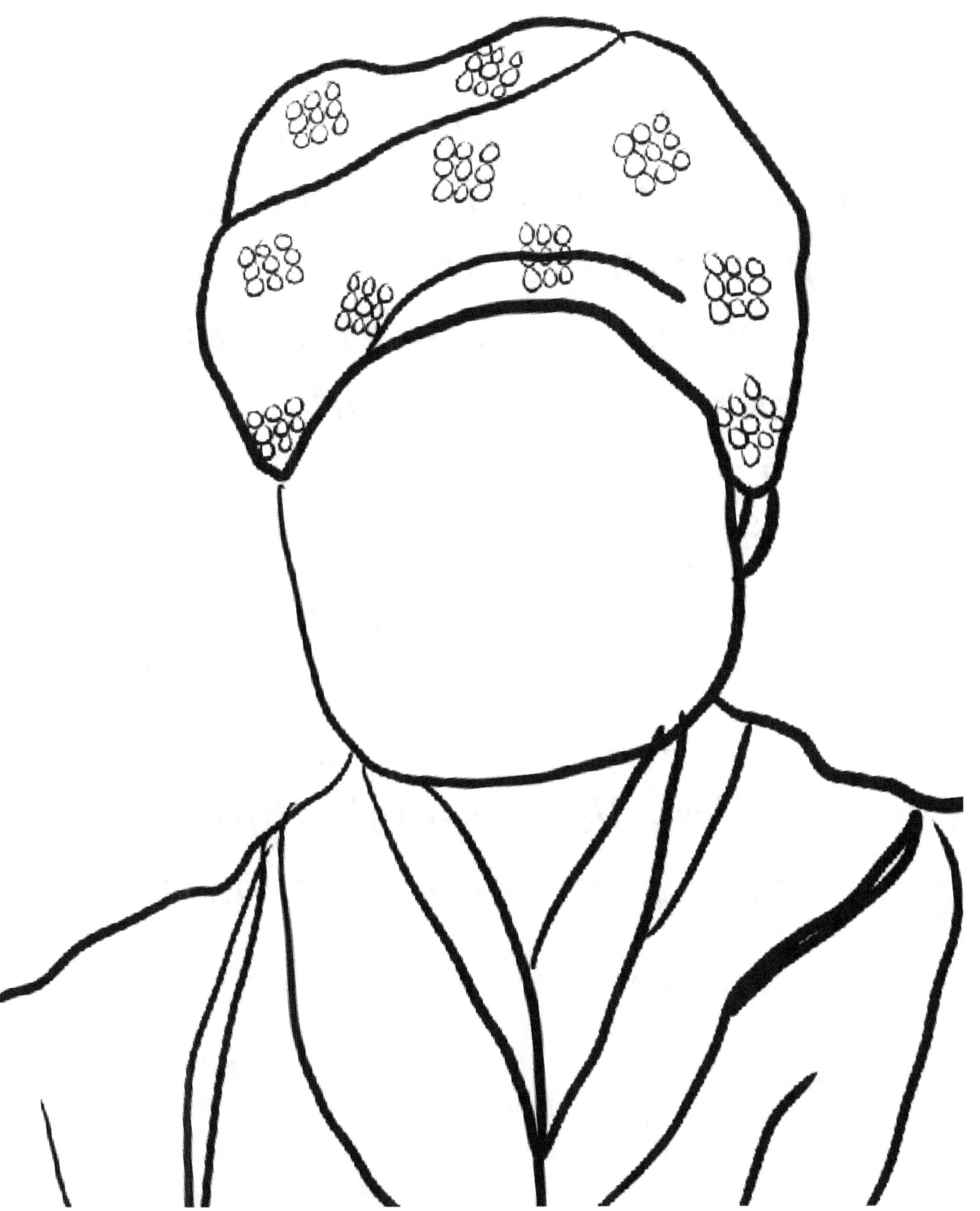

"I refused to take no for an answer. The air is the only place free from prejudice. I decided blacks should not have to experience the difficulties I had faced, so I decided to open a flying school and teach other black women to fly."

—Bessie Coleman
First Black Female Pilot/
First Native-American pilot

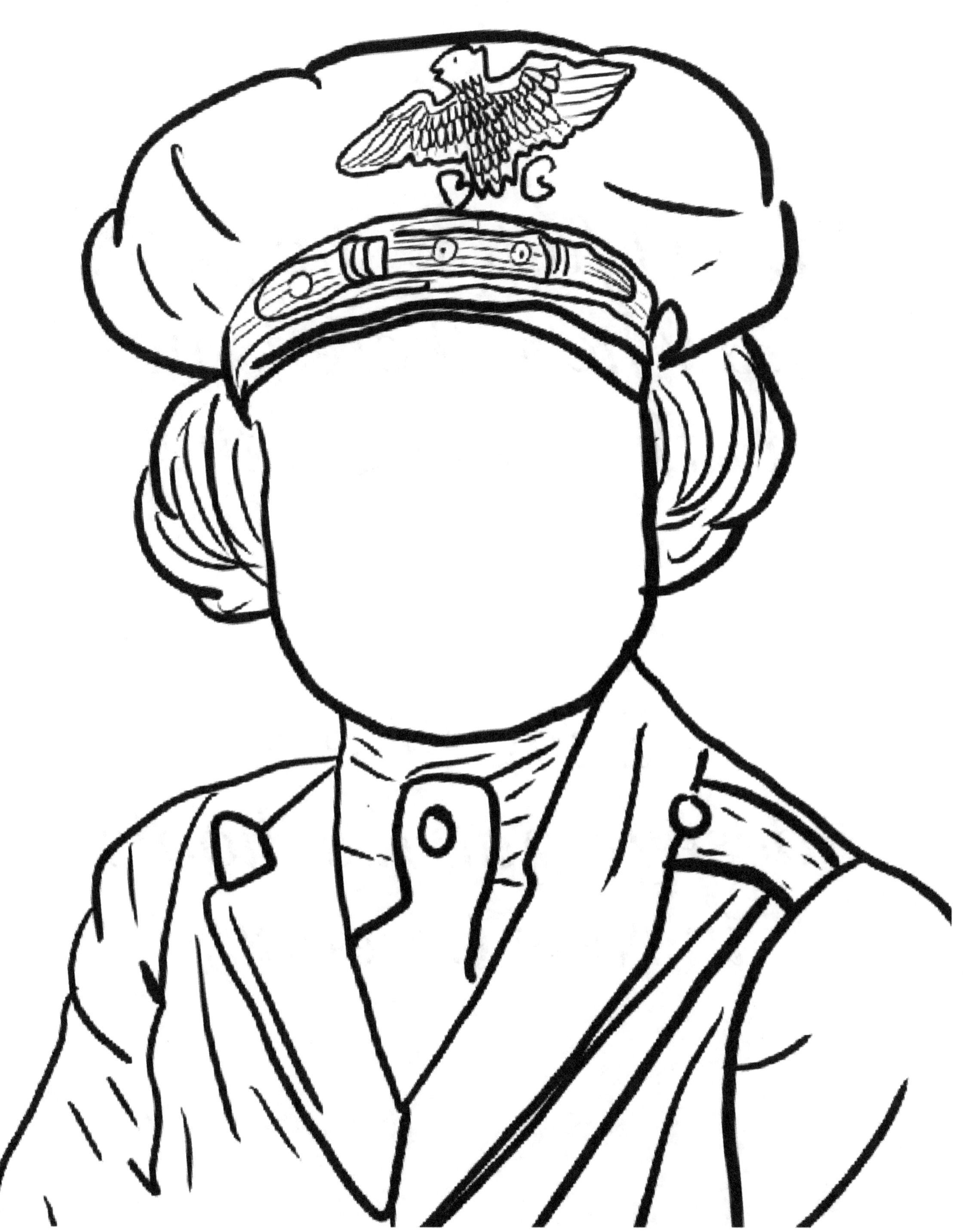

"Don't follow the path. Go where there is no path and begin the trail."

—Ruby Bridges (desegregated schools in New Orleans)

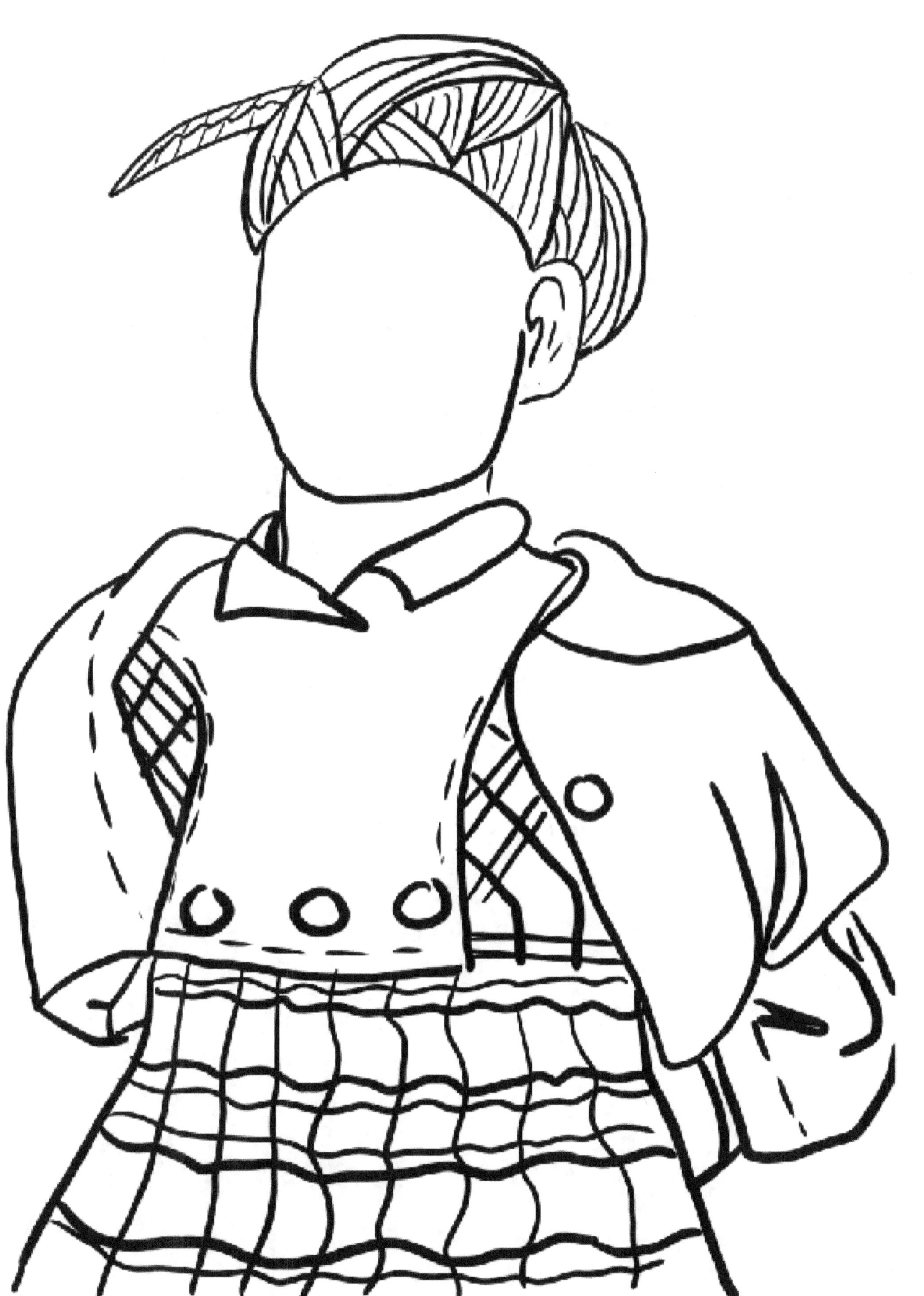

"I tell people I'm too stupid to know what's impossible. I have ridiculously large dreams, and half the time they come true."

—Debi Thomas
*U.S. Olympic Figure Skater/
Physician*

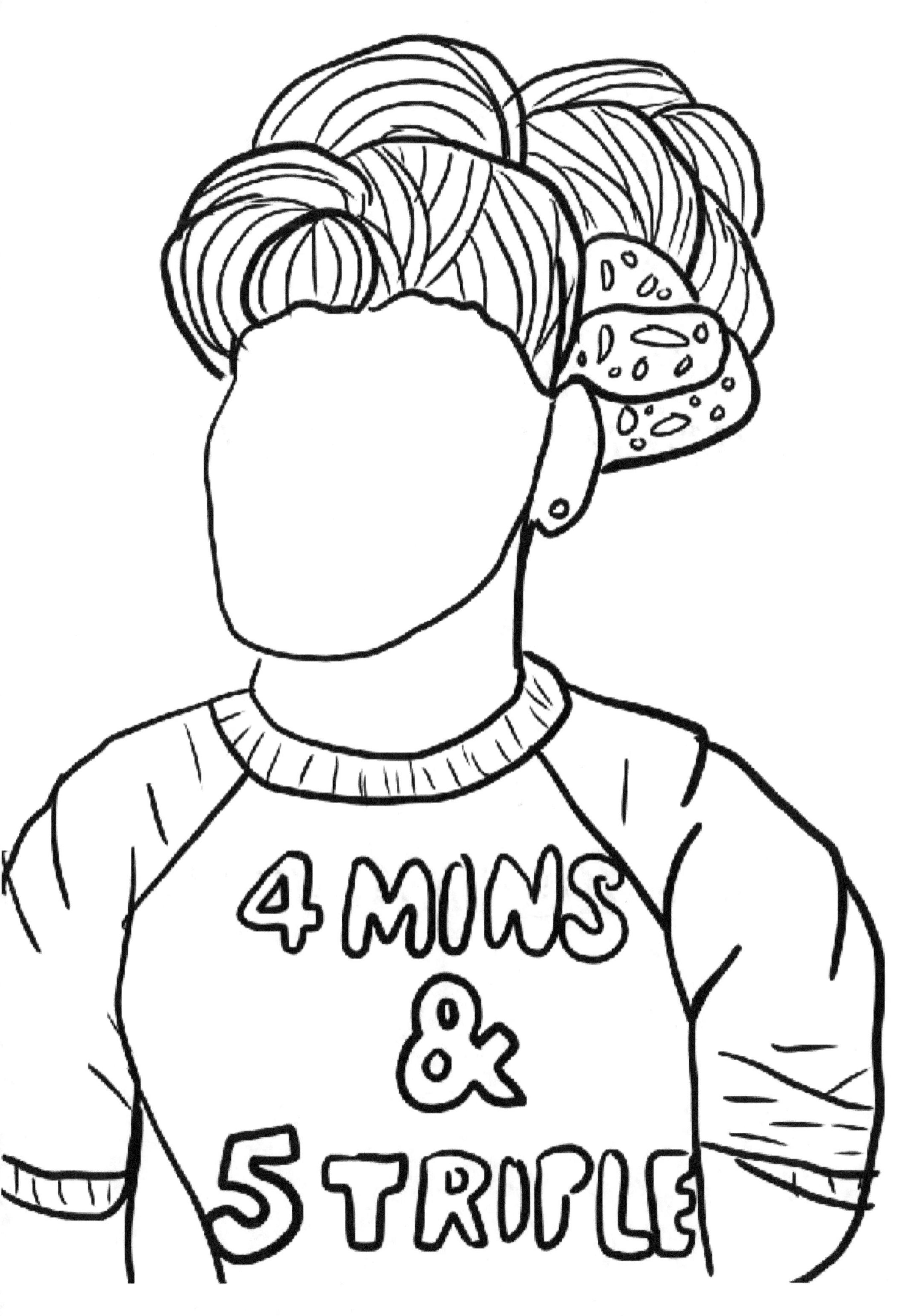

4 MINS
&
5 TRIPLE

"Each person must live
their life as a model for
others."

—Rosa Parks
Civil Rights Activist

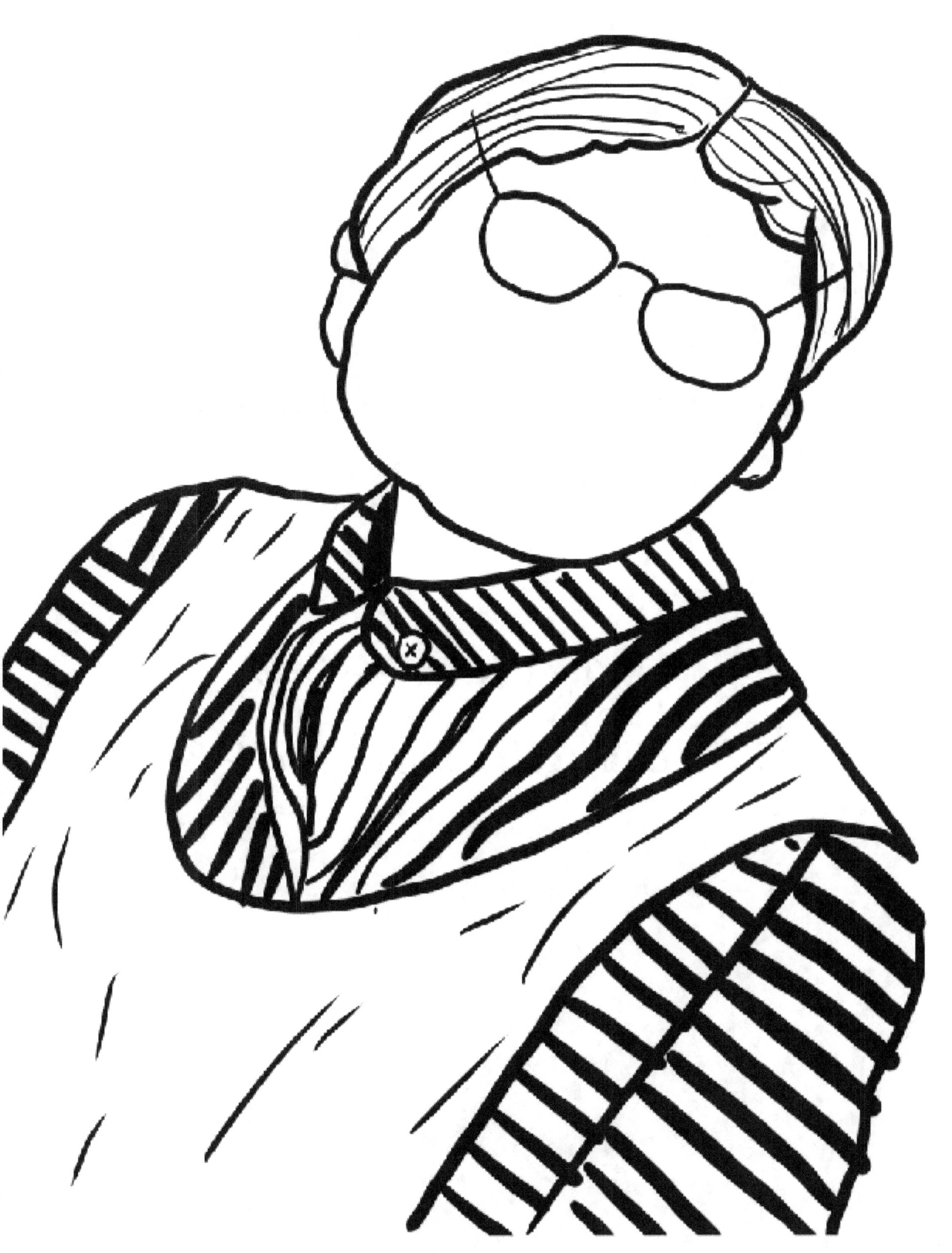

*"Nothing will work
unless you do."*

*—Maya Angelo
Writer/Activist/Singer*

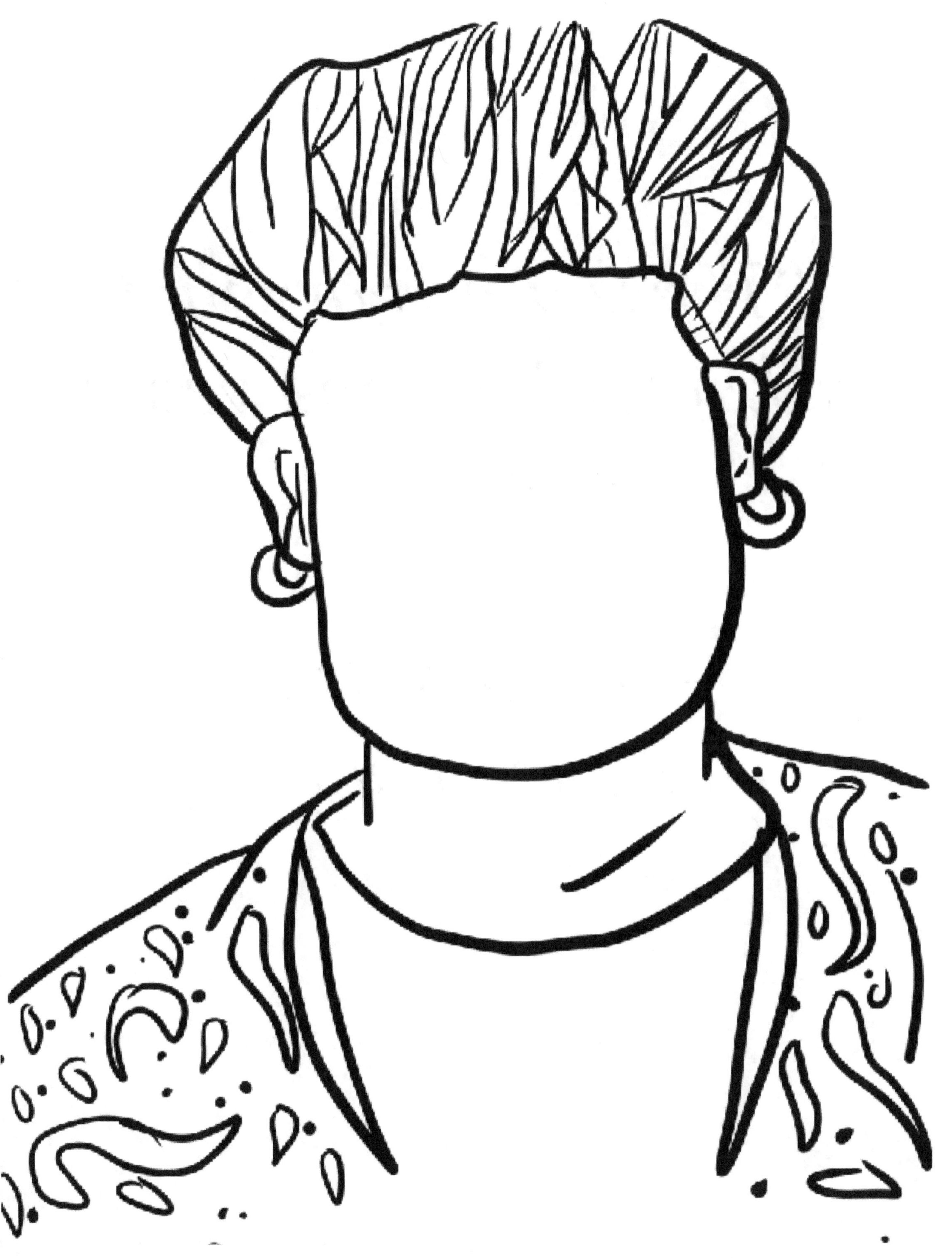

"There are years that ask questions and years that answer."

—Zora Nelson
(American author)

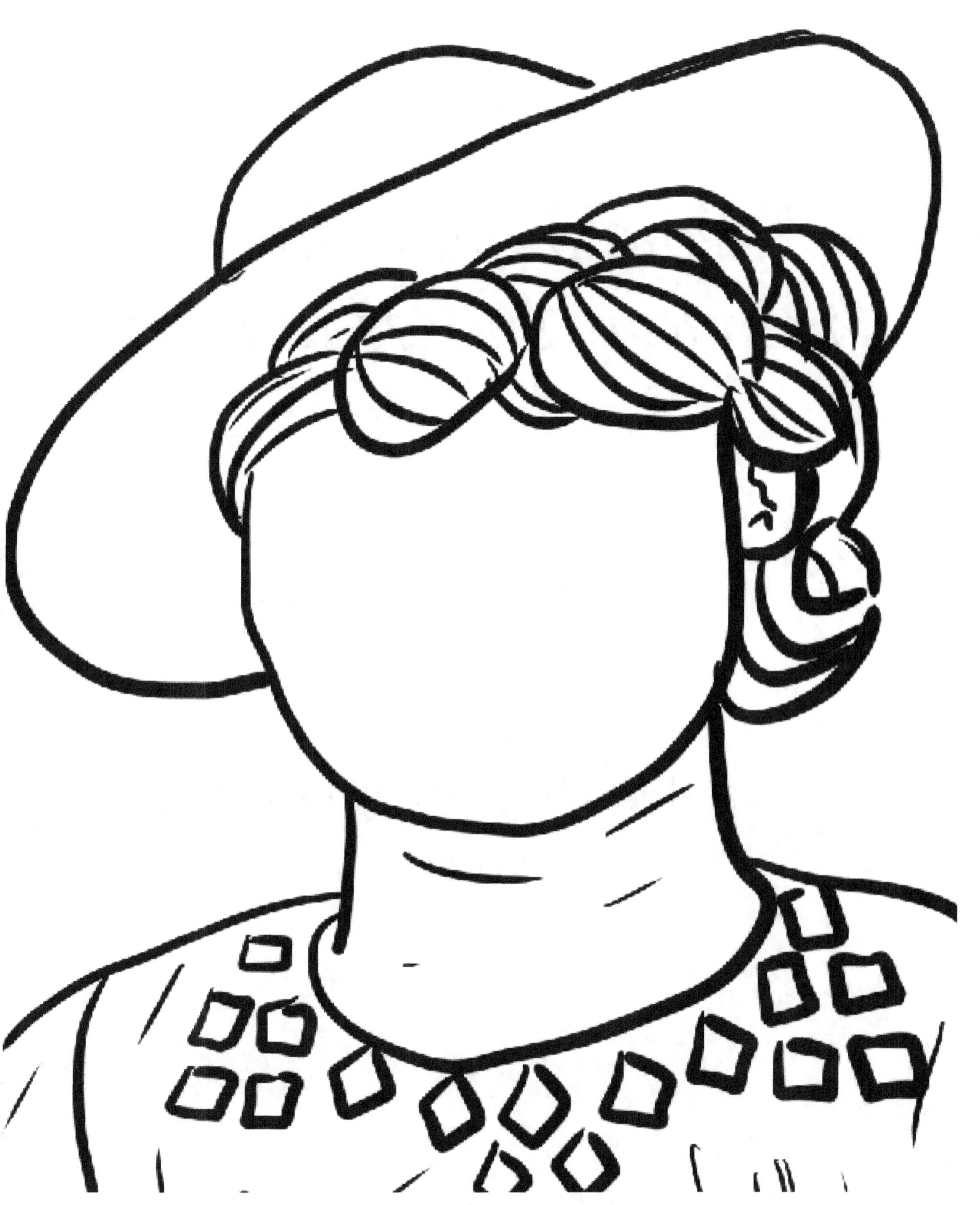

"Avoid popularity. It has many snares and no real benefit."

—Dorothy Dandridge
Singer/Actress
first black woman nominated for an Academy Award for best actress

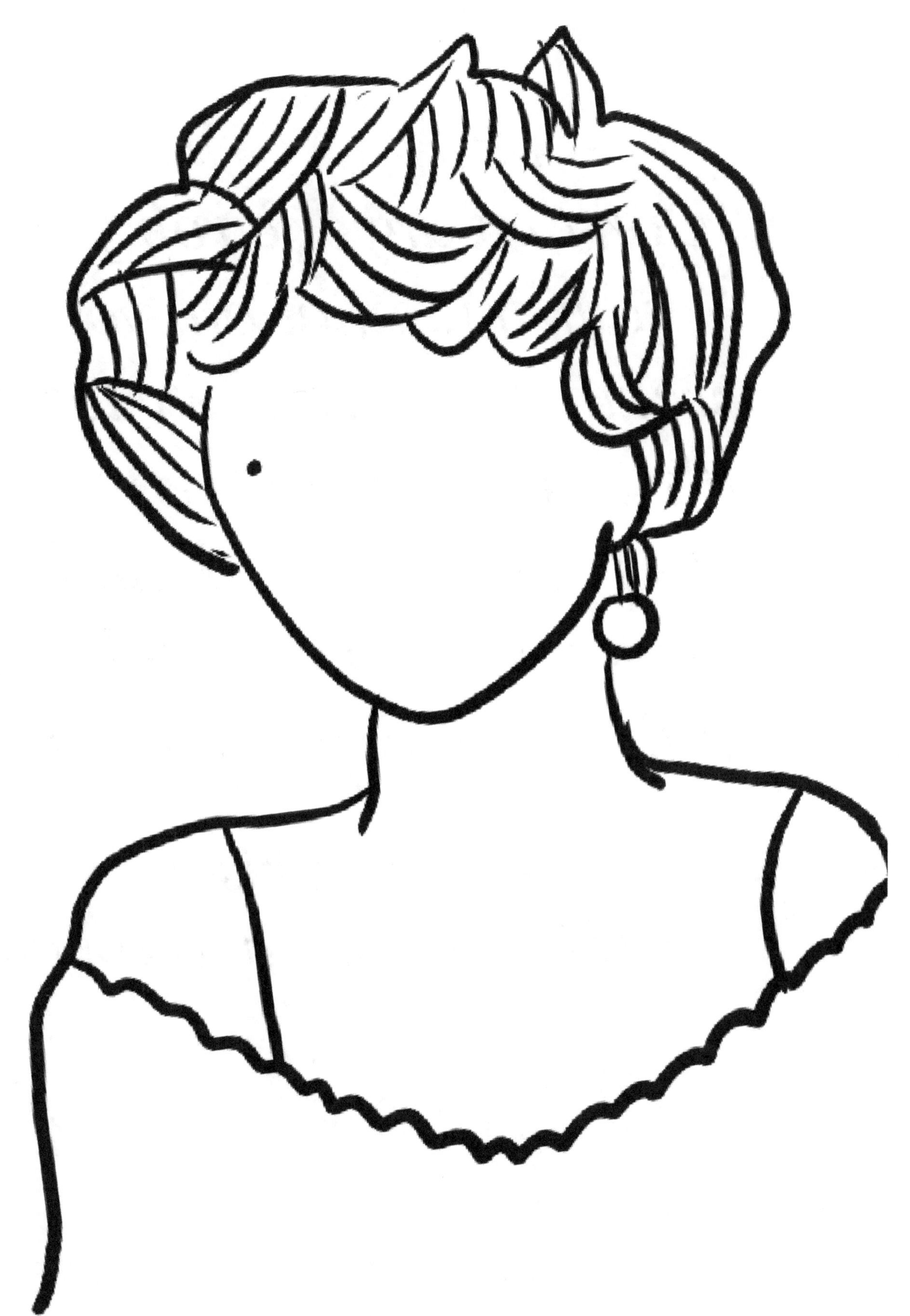

"Don't let anyone rob you of your imagination, your creativity, or your curiosity. It's your place in the world; it's your life. Go on and do all you can with it, and make it the life you want to live."

—Mae Jemison
First black woman astronaut

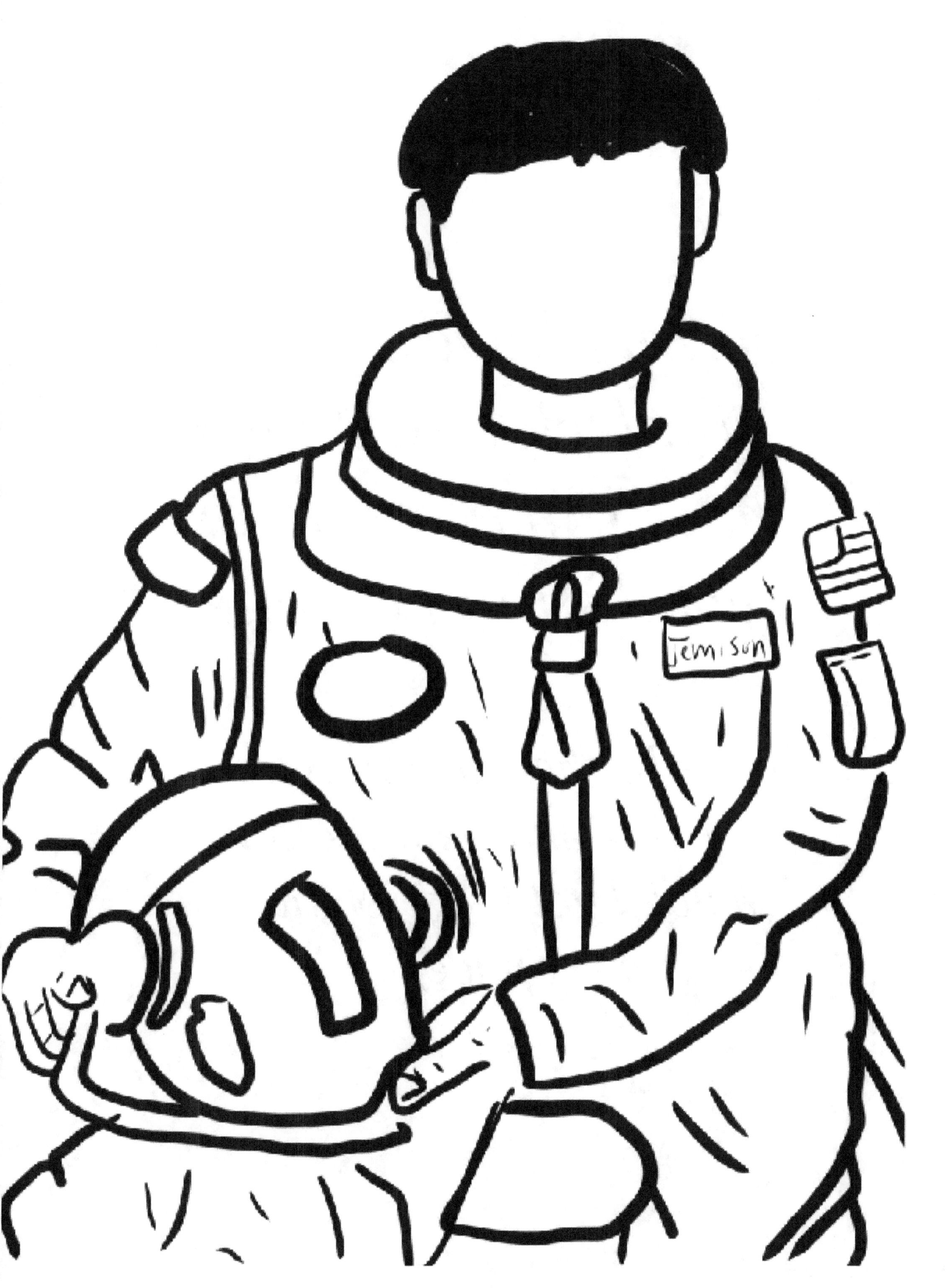

Jemison

"I don't have a feeling of inferiority. Never had. I'm as good as anybody, but no better."

—Katherine Johnson
NASA mathematician
(helped get the first man in
space)

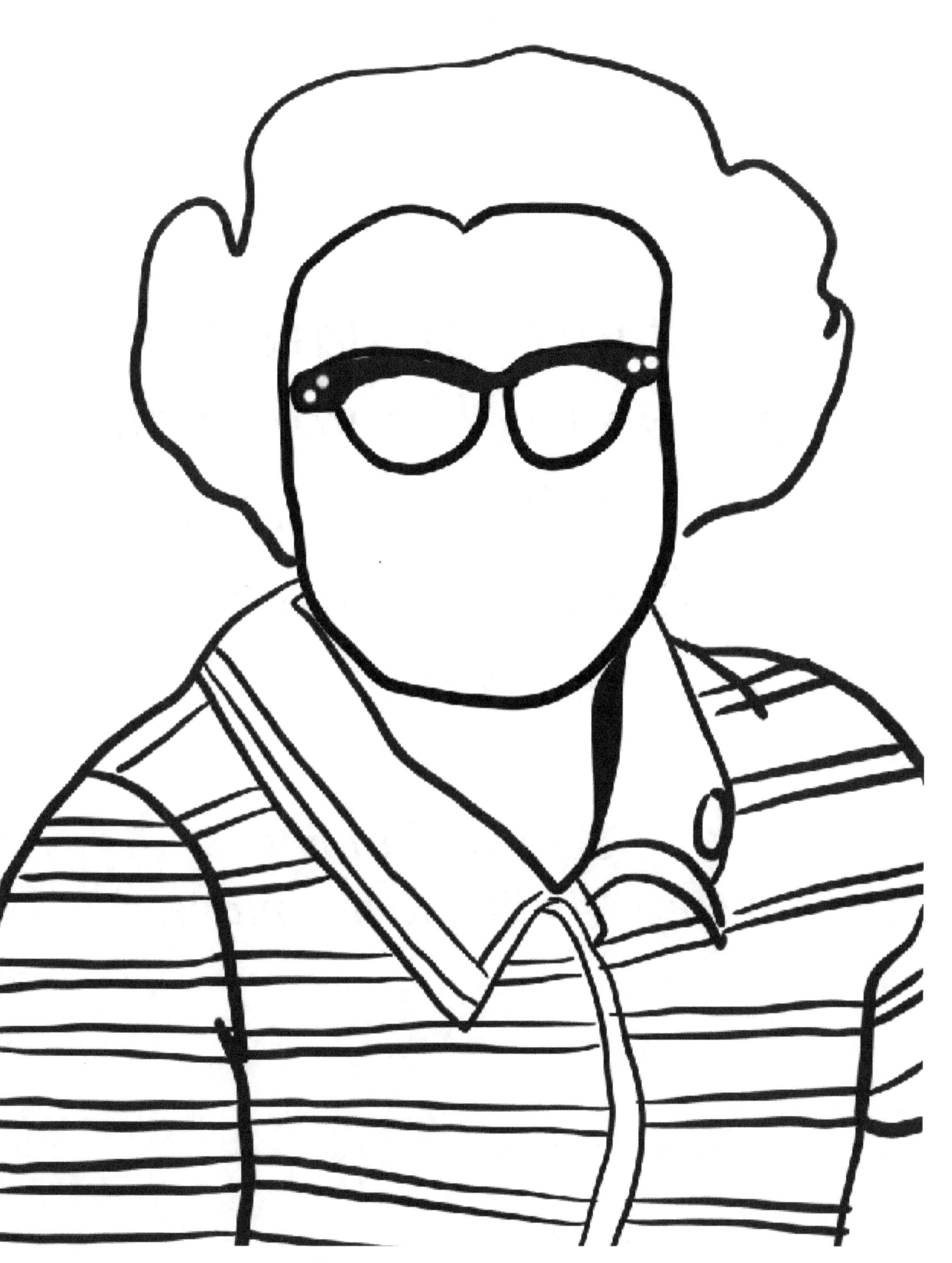

"I think you have to love yourself before you fall in love. I'm still learning to love myself."

—*Serena Williams*
Award winning tennis player

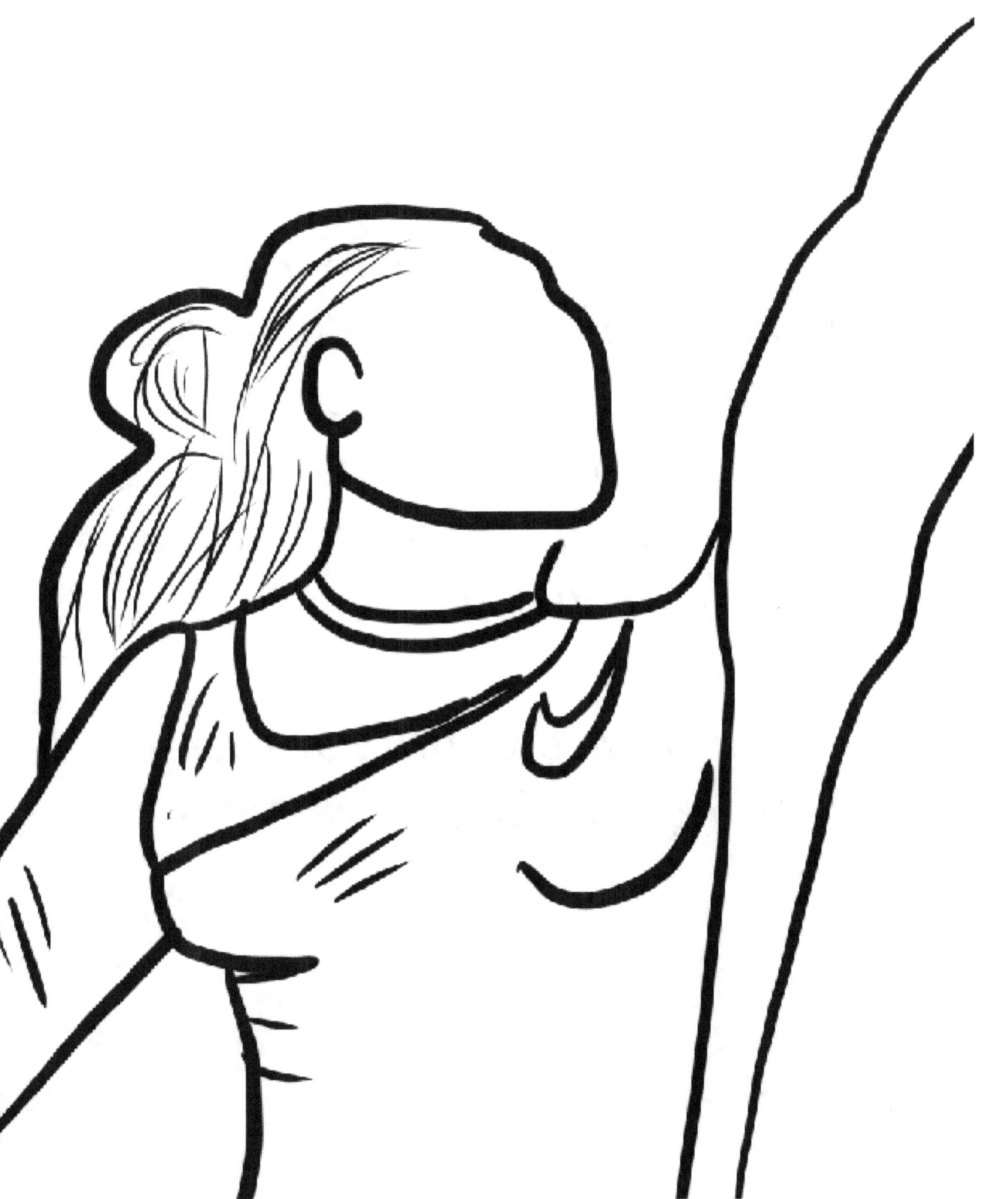

"I love working with kids, talking with them and listening to them. I always encourage kids to reach beyond their dreams. Don't try to be like me. Be better than me."

—Florence Griffith Joyner
Track and Filed Olympians

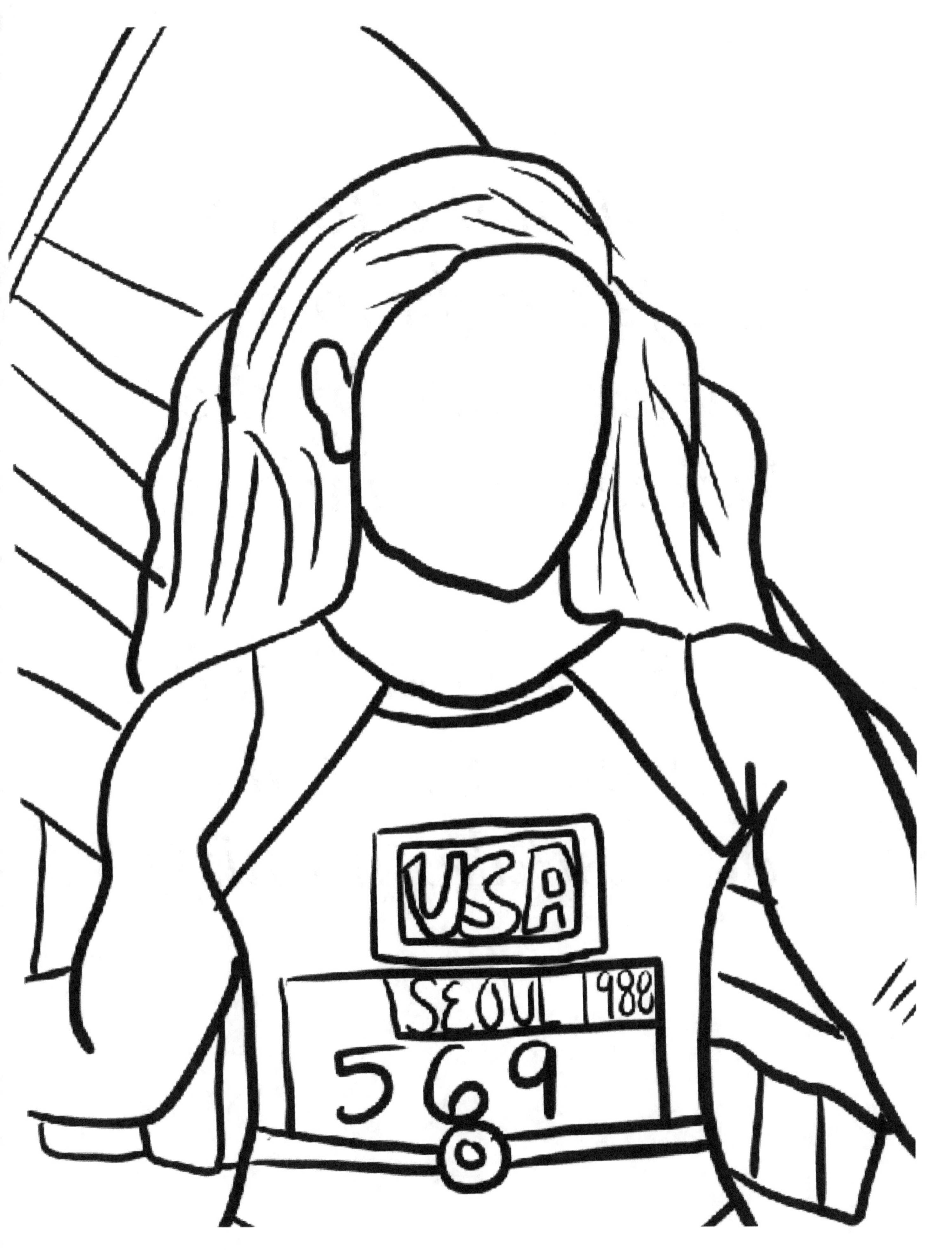
USA
SEOUL 1988
569

"I will not allow my life's light to be determined by the darkness around me."

—Sojourner Truth (women's rights activist/abolitionist)

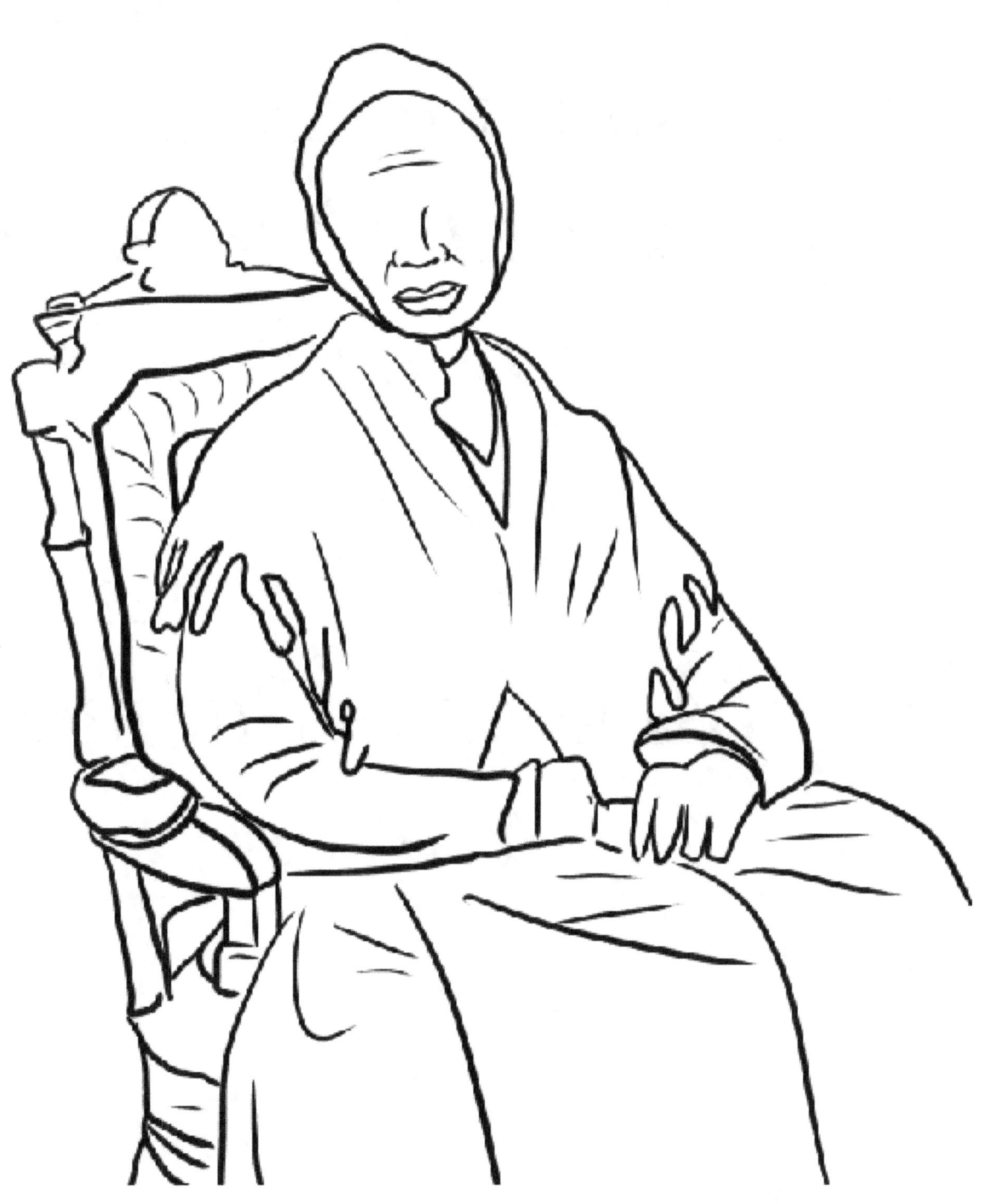

"Follow your heart's truth with no need for personal gain other than the feeling produced when doing what you truly love."

—Keke Palmer (American Singer/ Actress)

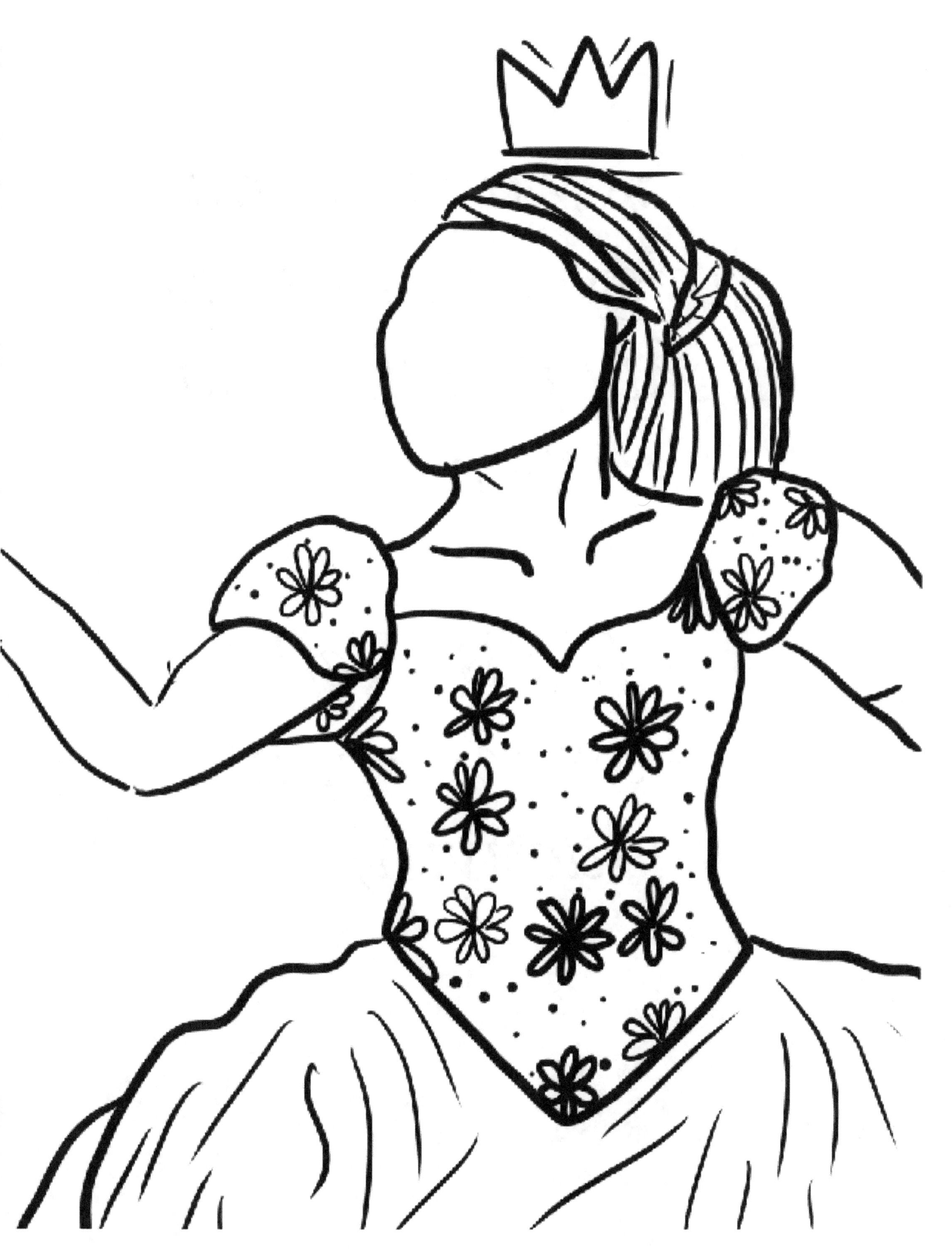

"The way to right wrongs is to turn the light of truth upon them."

—Ida B. Wells (women's rights activist)

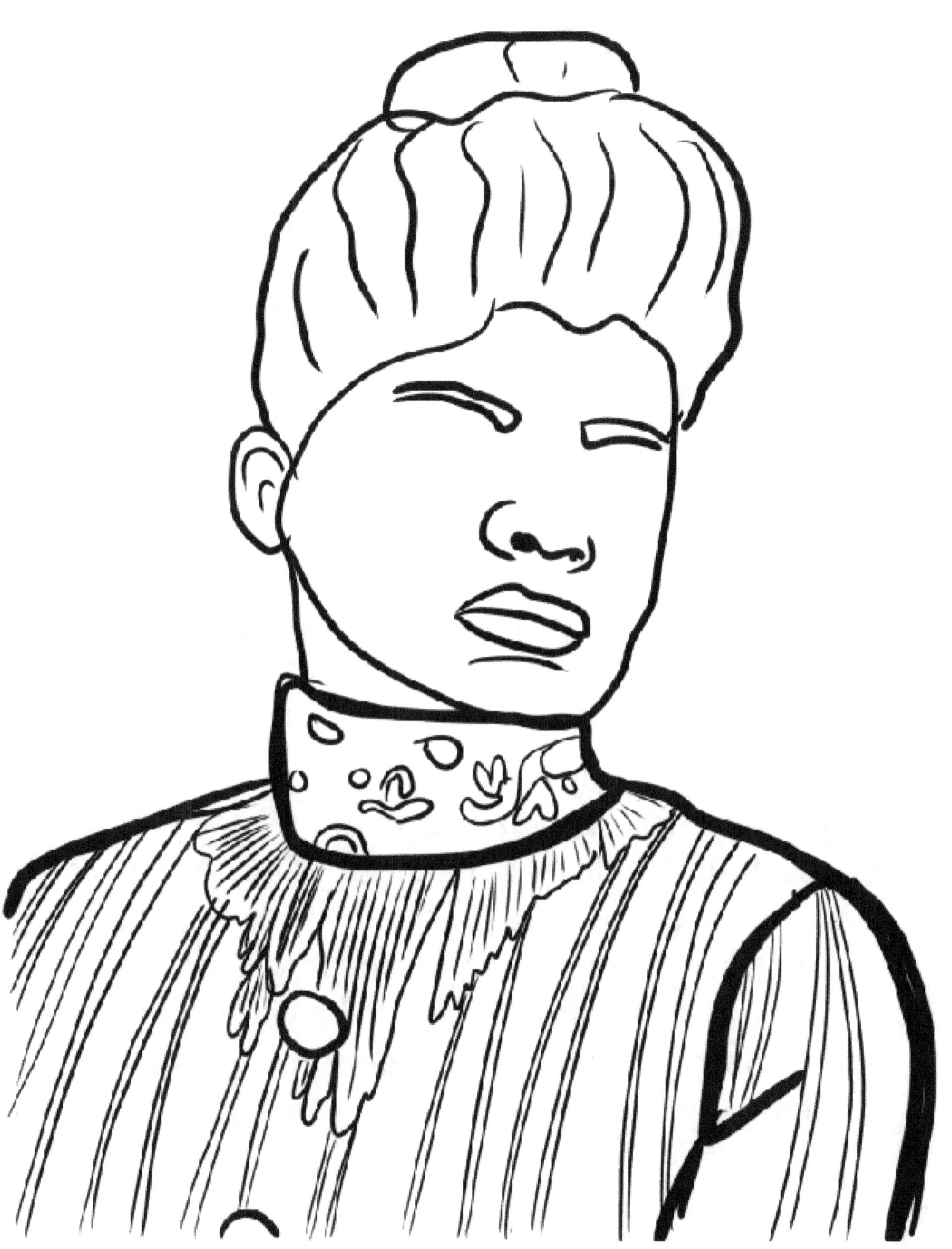

Those who are doing it now...

When I started creating this coloring book for you I asked black women to send me pictures of them, their kids, and their inspirations. The people in this section know what it's like to hate themselves and to struggle. They helped me make this book because they know how hard it is and they wanted to make growing up easier for you. This section is to prove to you that black women all over the country who don't know you love you. Being a black woman is scary but it's the biggest and most intimate sisterhood you can have.

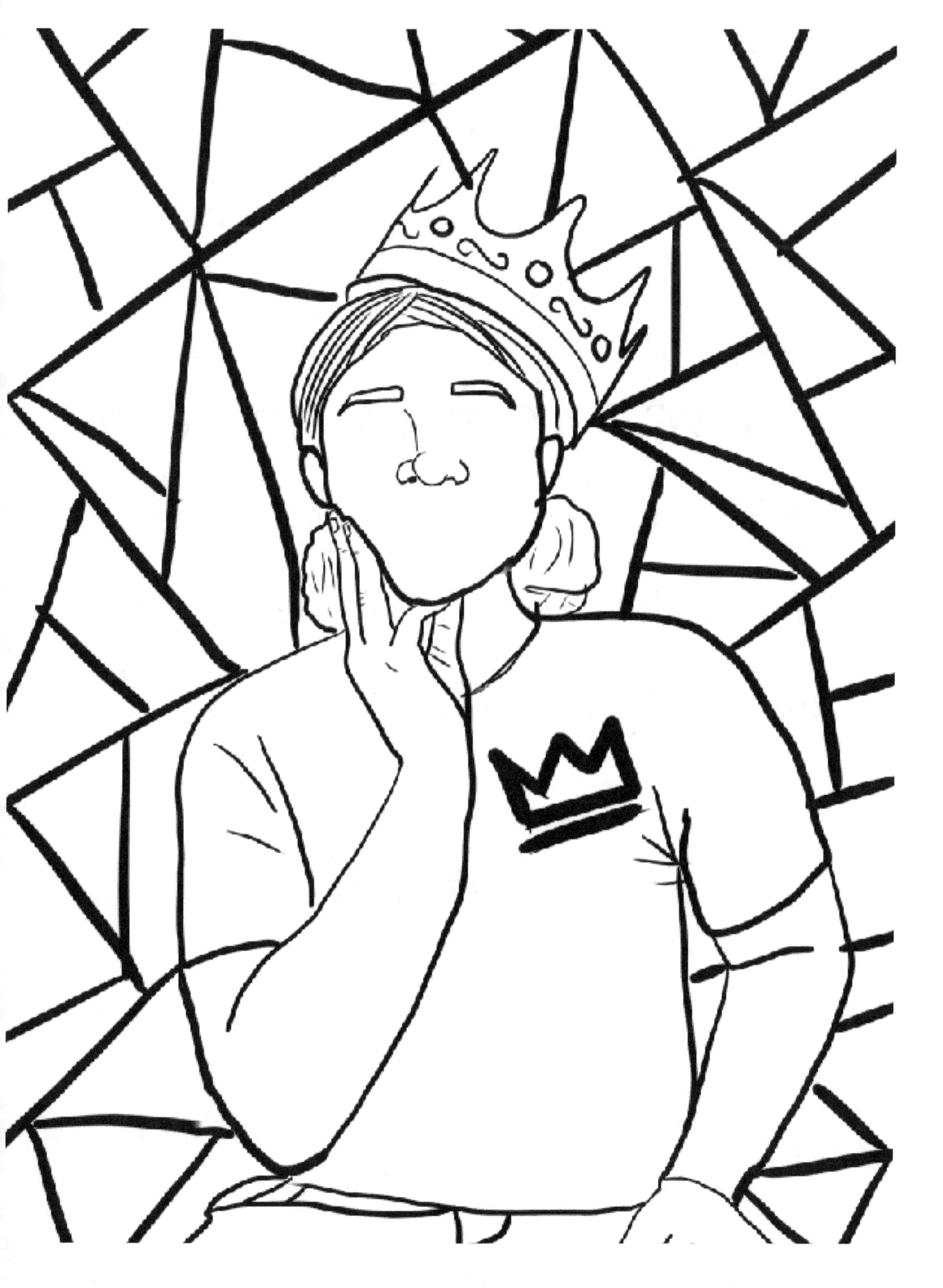

"Give to others without expecting anything in return and watch how your life will flourish."

—Naomi

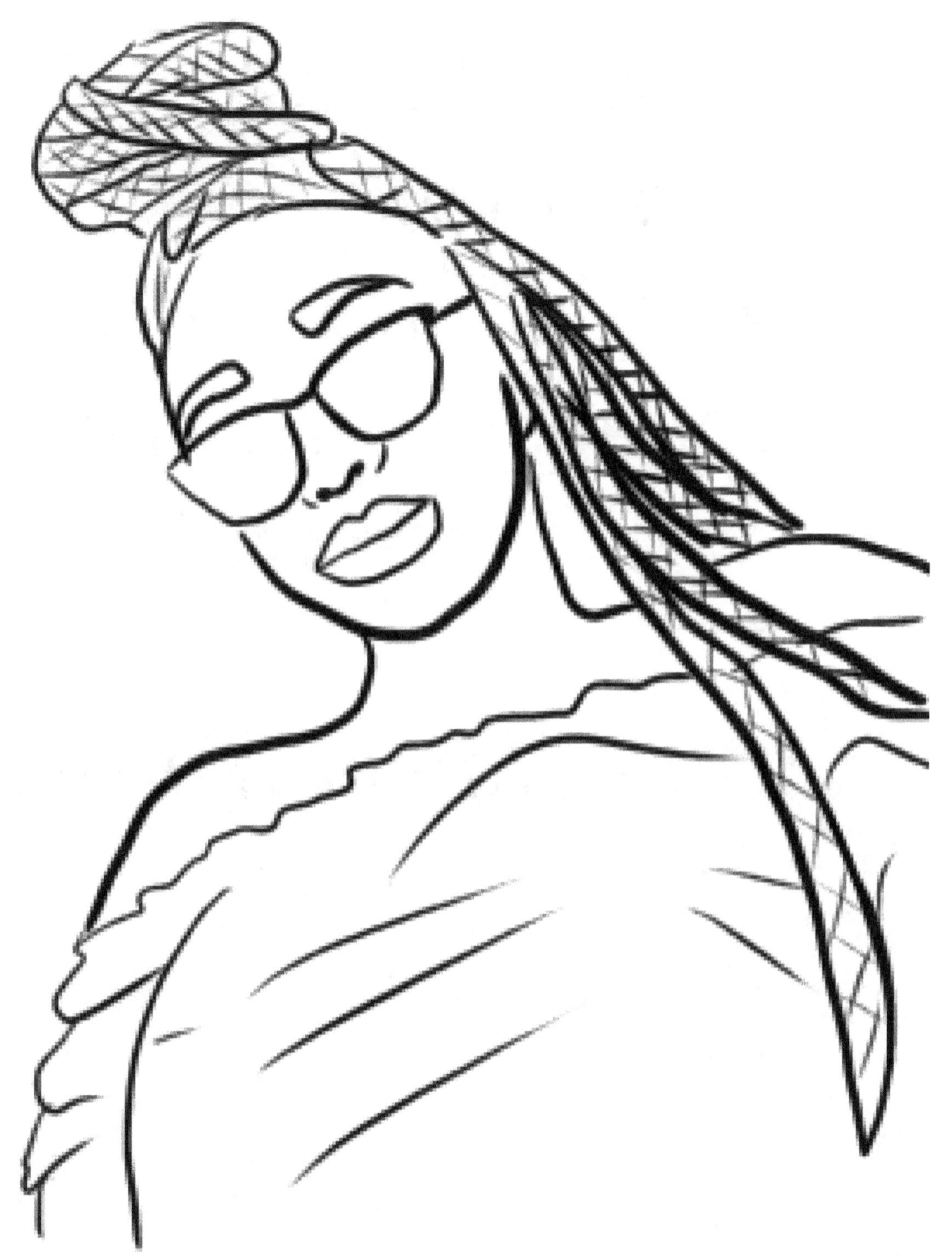

"Your heritage is rich and your roots run deep. Follow them and you will rediscover your crown."

—Naomi Winston

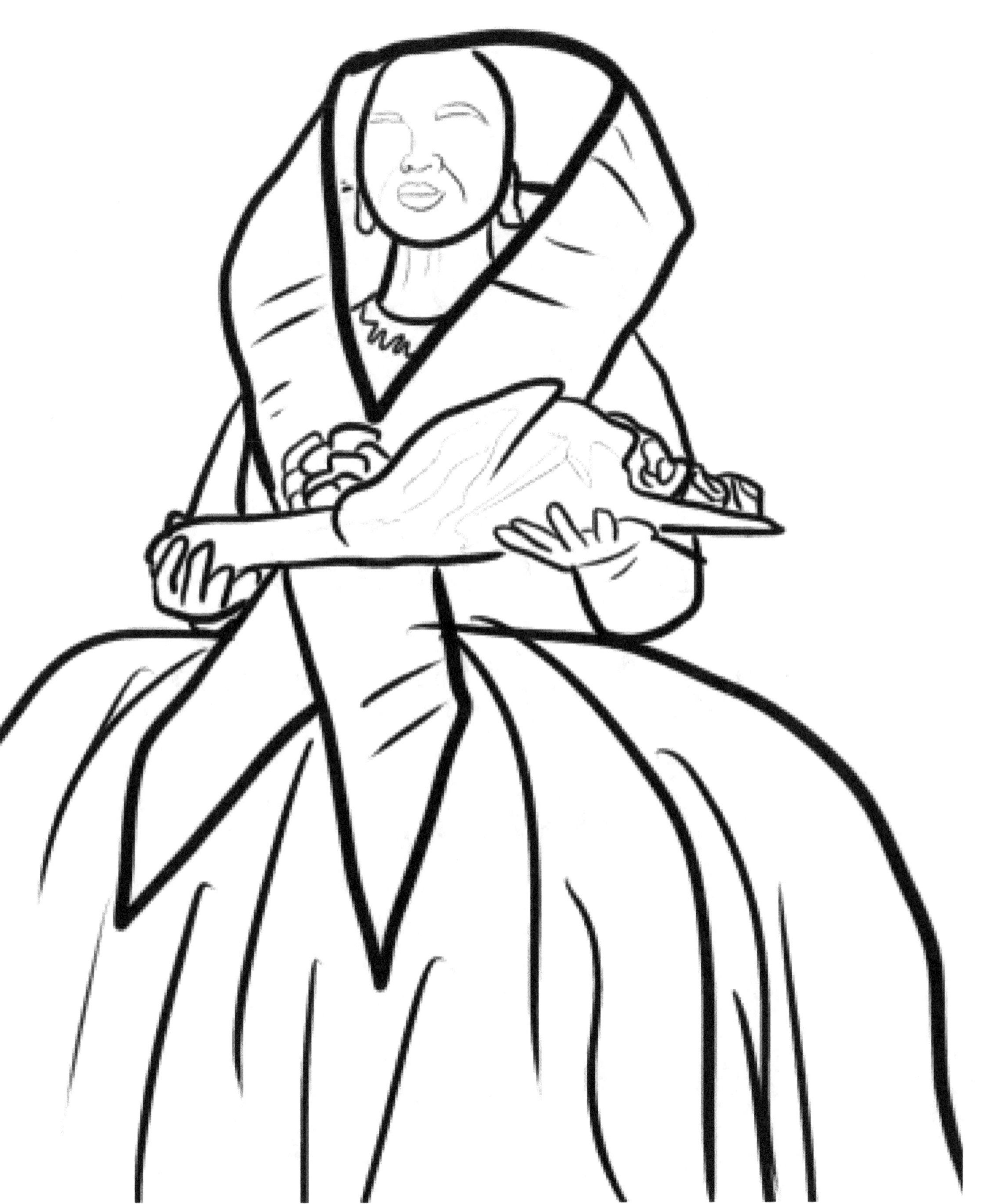

My Past
≠
My Future
and Neither does
yours

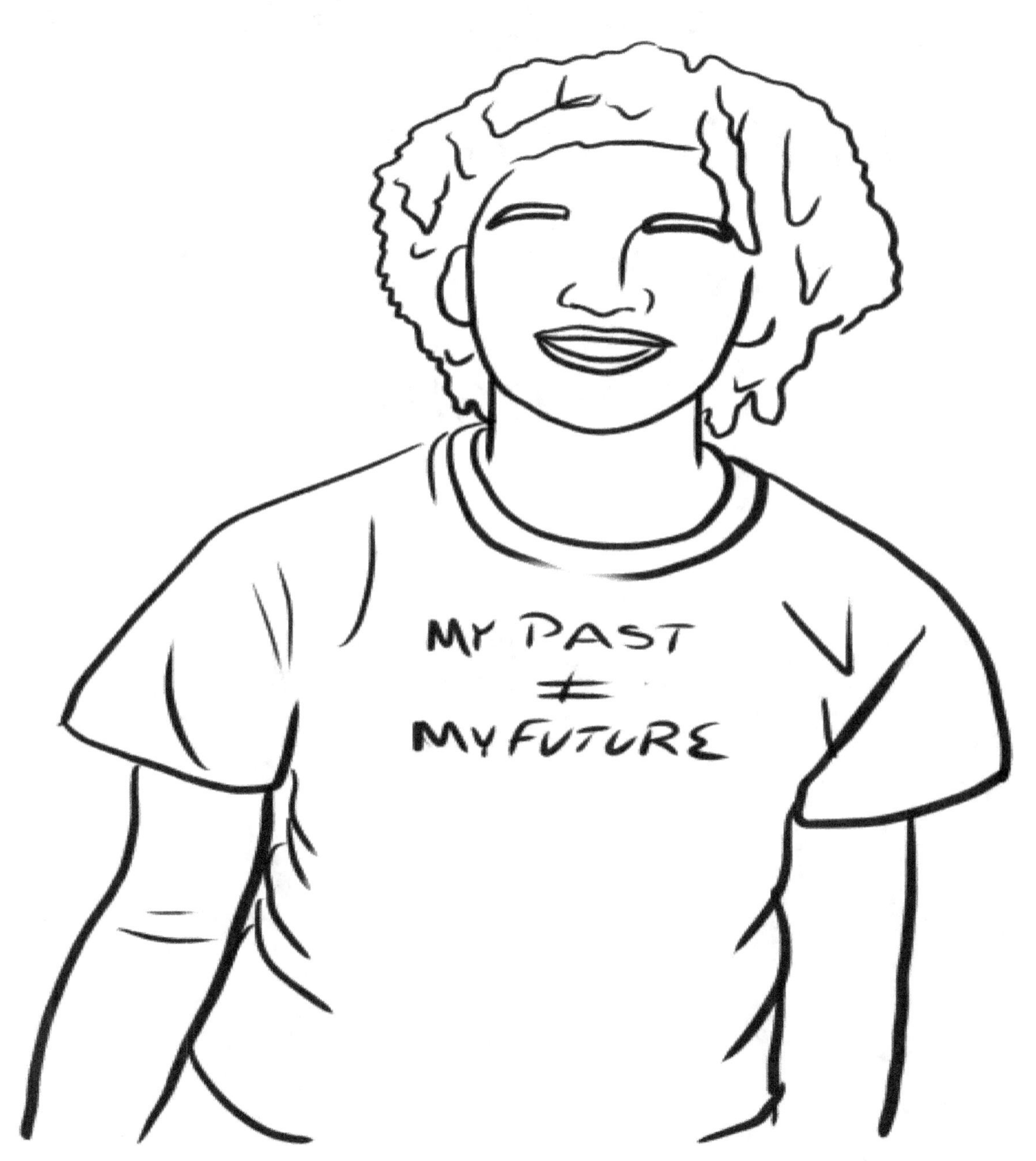

MY PAST
≠
MY FUTURE

"*Break generational curses. Teach your kids love without hitting them.*"

—Naomi

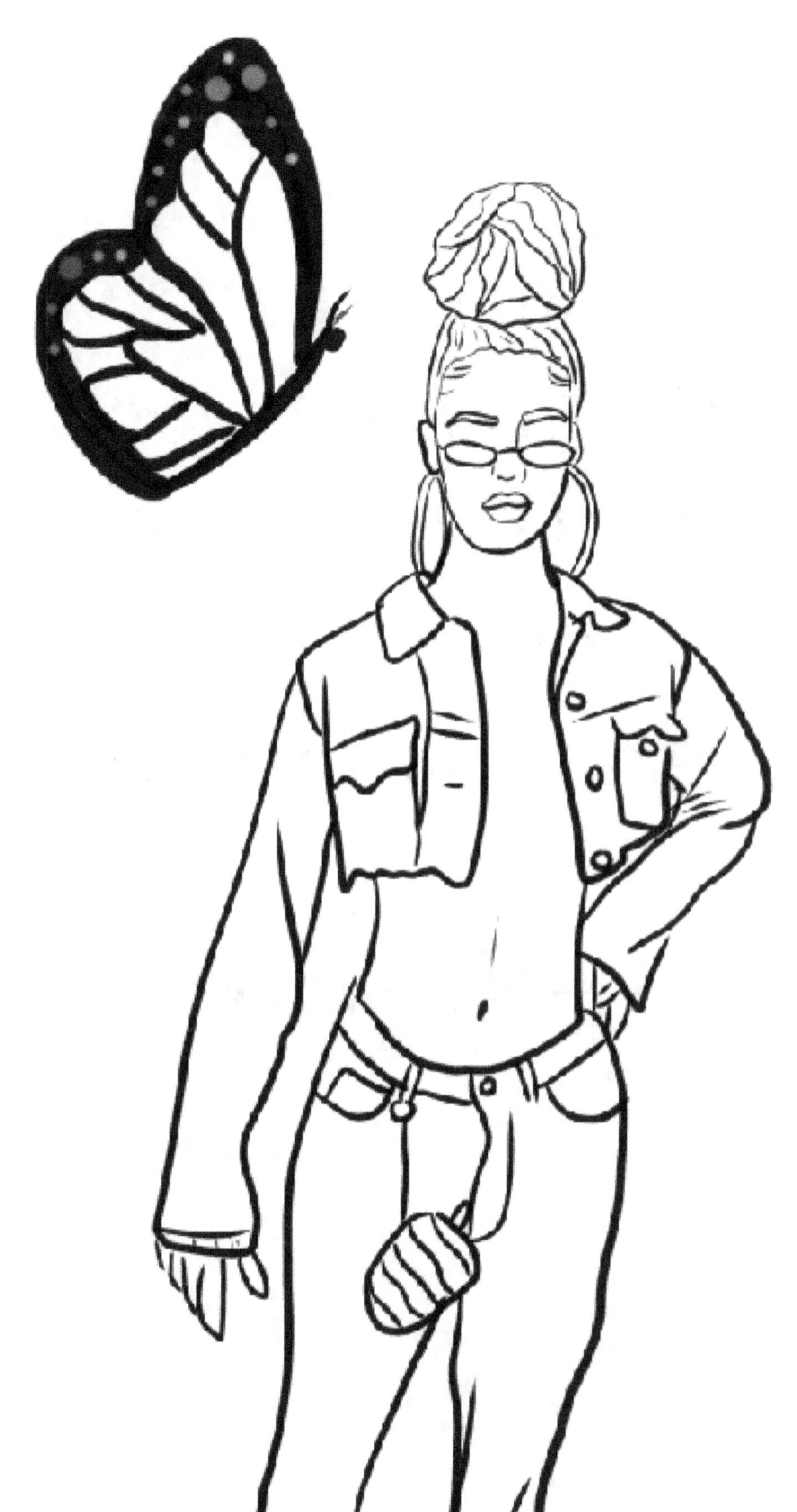

" *Take care of yourself. Be kind to yourself. Be patient with yourself. Flowers take time to grow and so do you.*"

—Naomi Winston

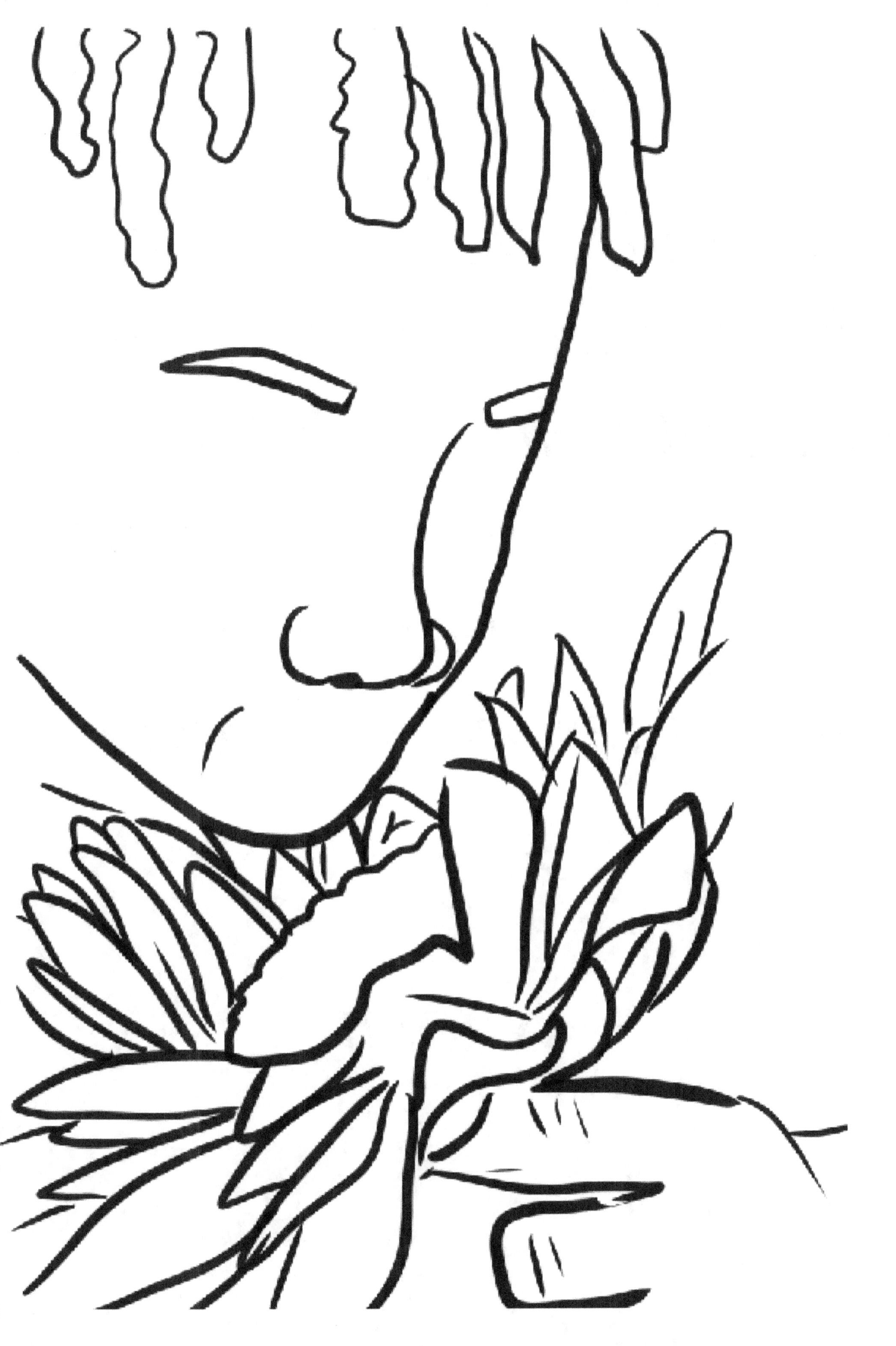

"*Even if you may never hear it from those who it would matter the most from, I'm sorry. Some of us are waiting from apologies we will never get*"

—*Naomi*

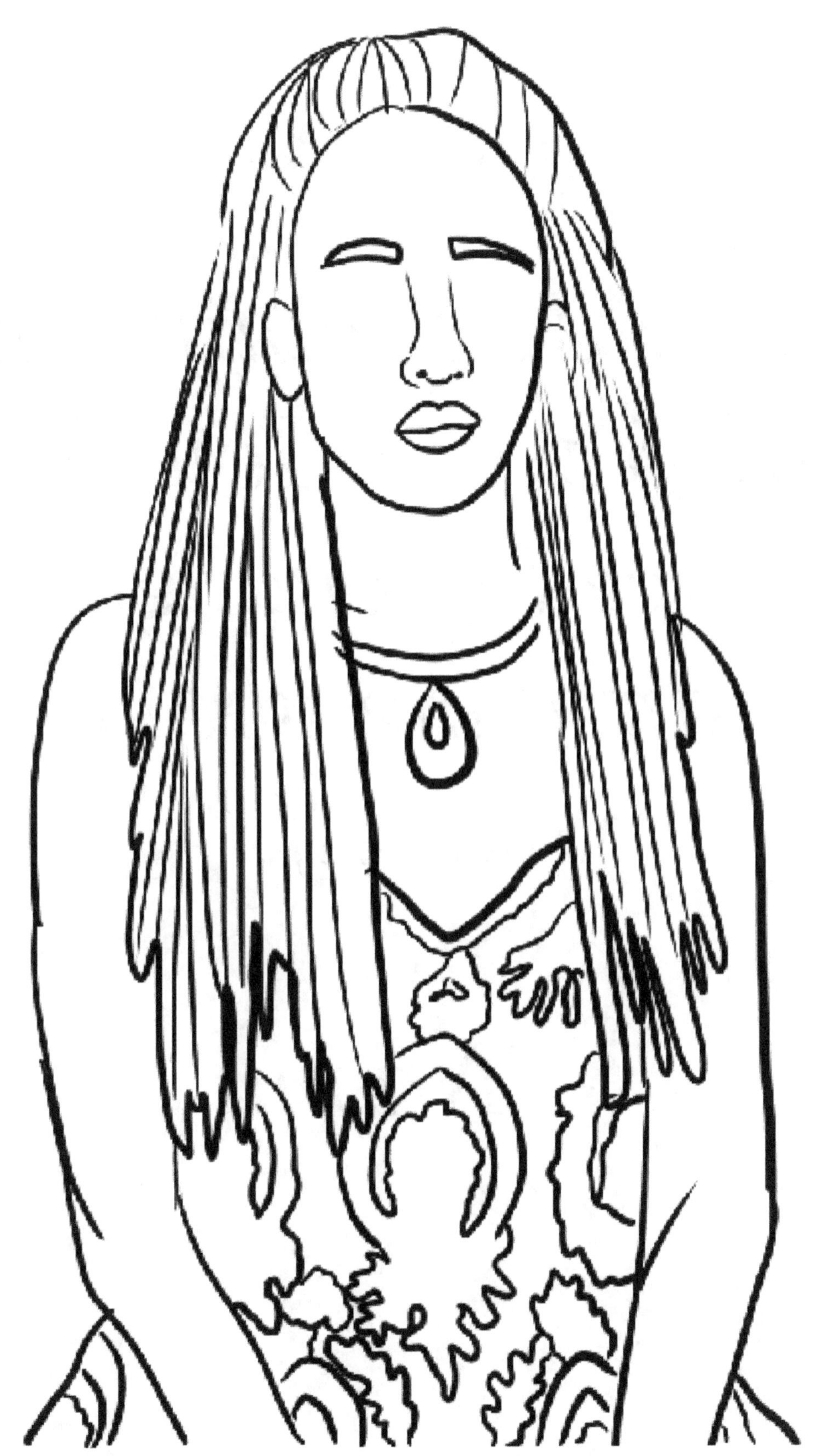

"*You are beautiful the way you are. You don't need to change anything about yourself.*"

—*Naomi*

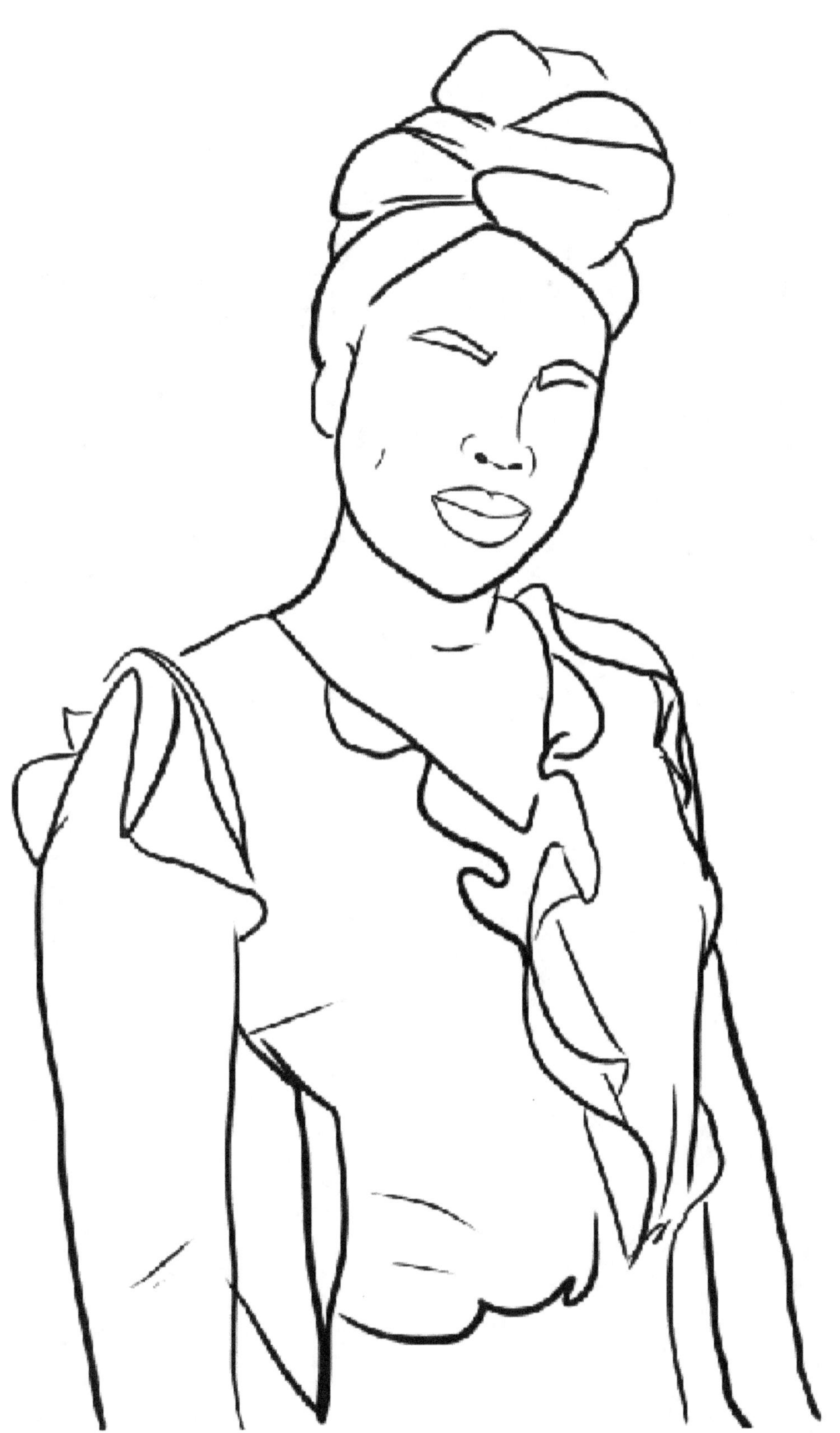

"If you don't love the image you see in the mirror then work to like yourself first."

—Naomi

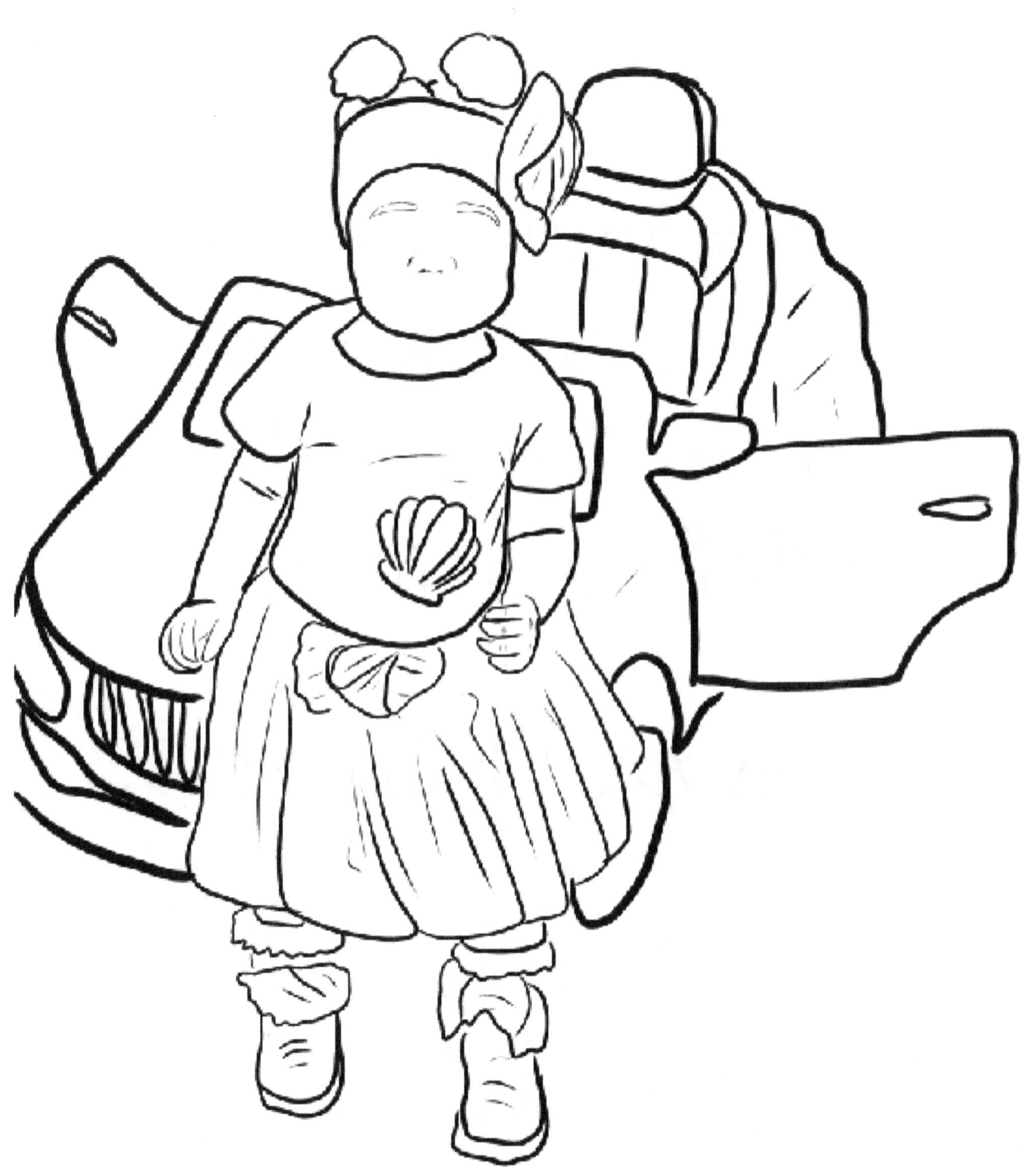

"Adventure waits for you. Don't wait to travel. The world is made for you to see."

—Naomi Winston

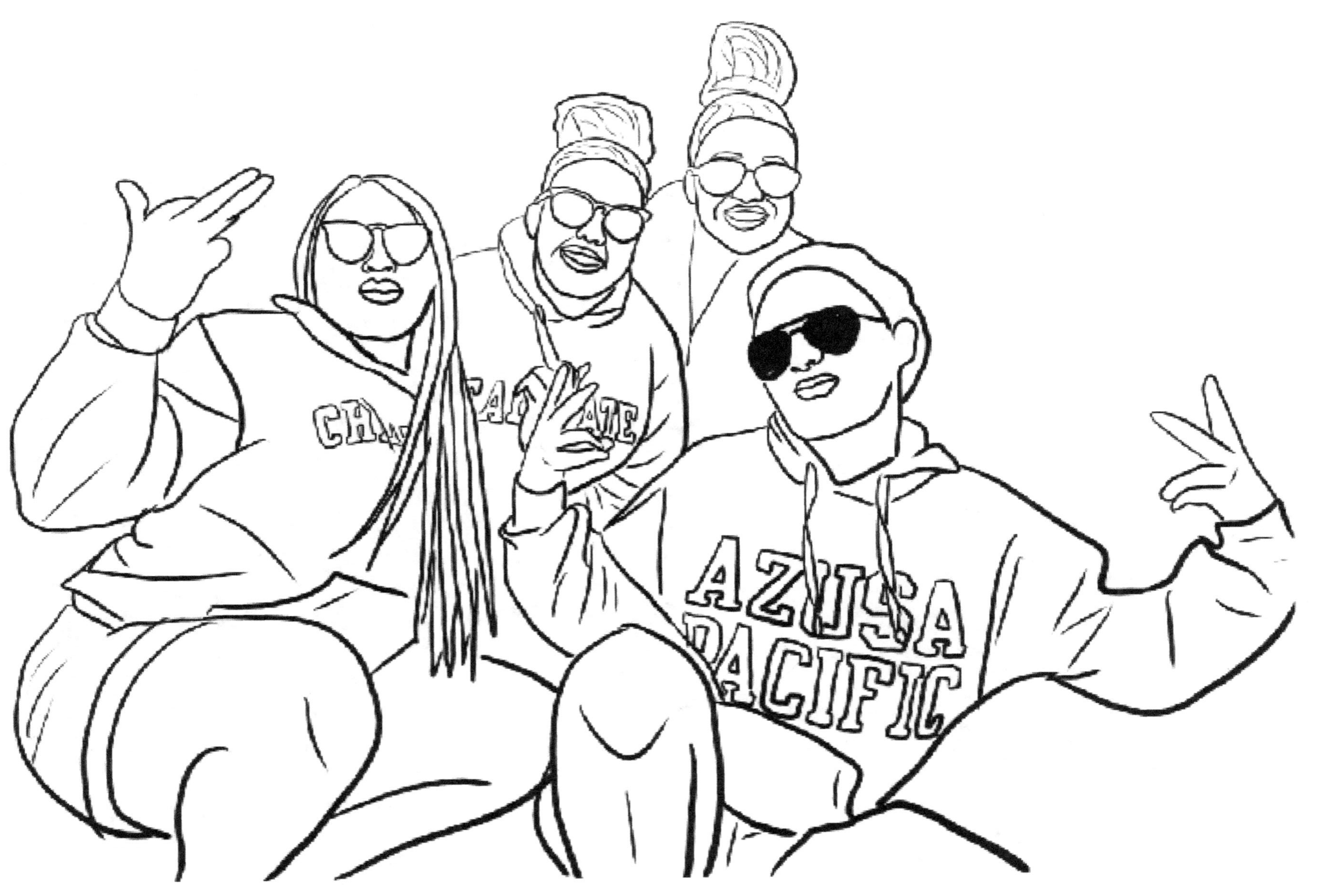

AZUSA
PACIFIC

"*Love shouldn't hurt.*"

—Naomi

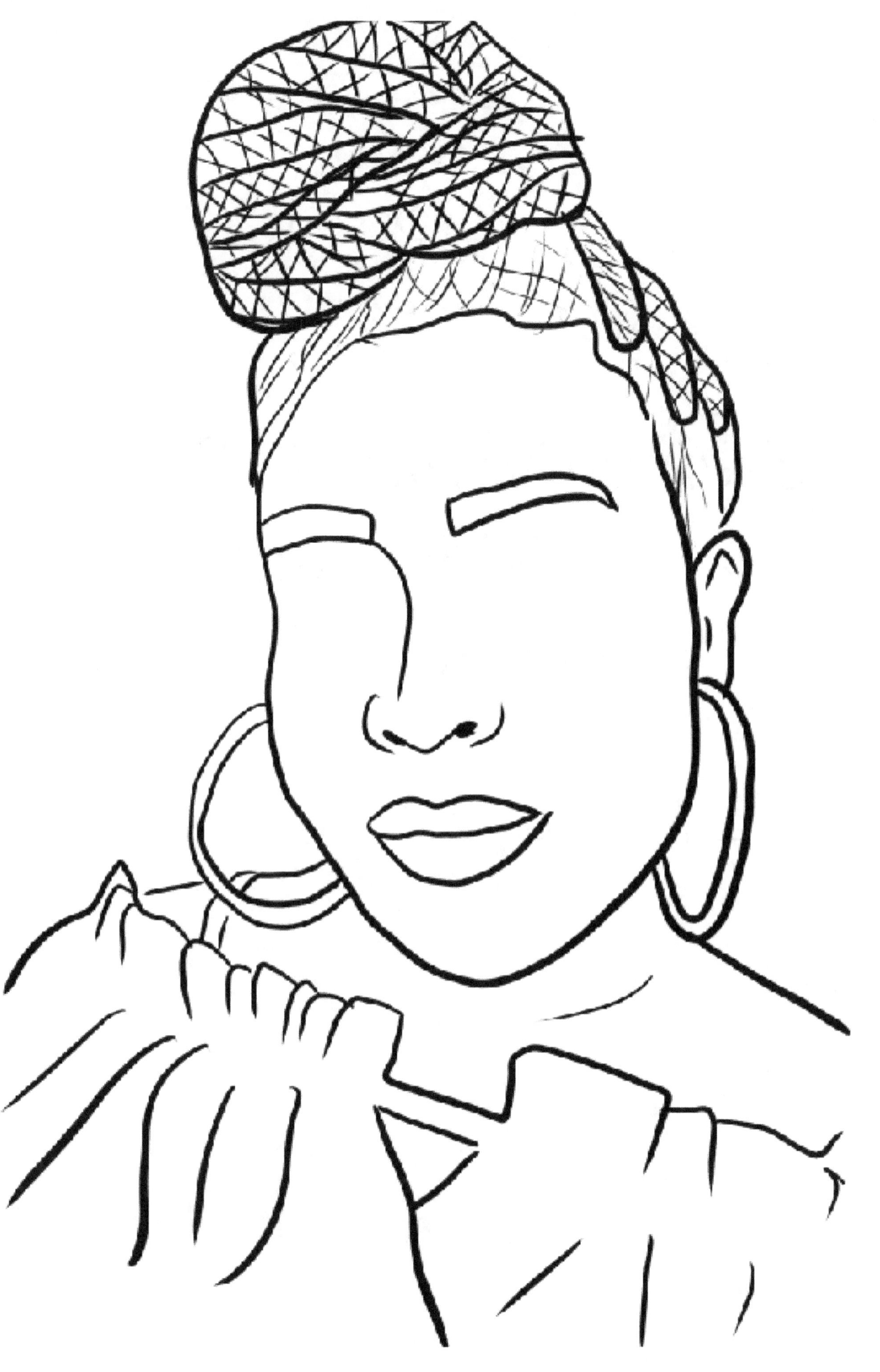

"Seeing the future. See your visions and pursuing it."

—Naomi Winston

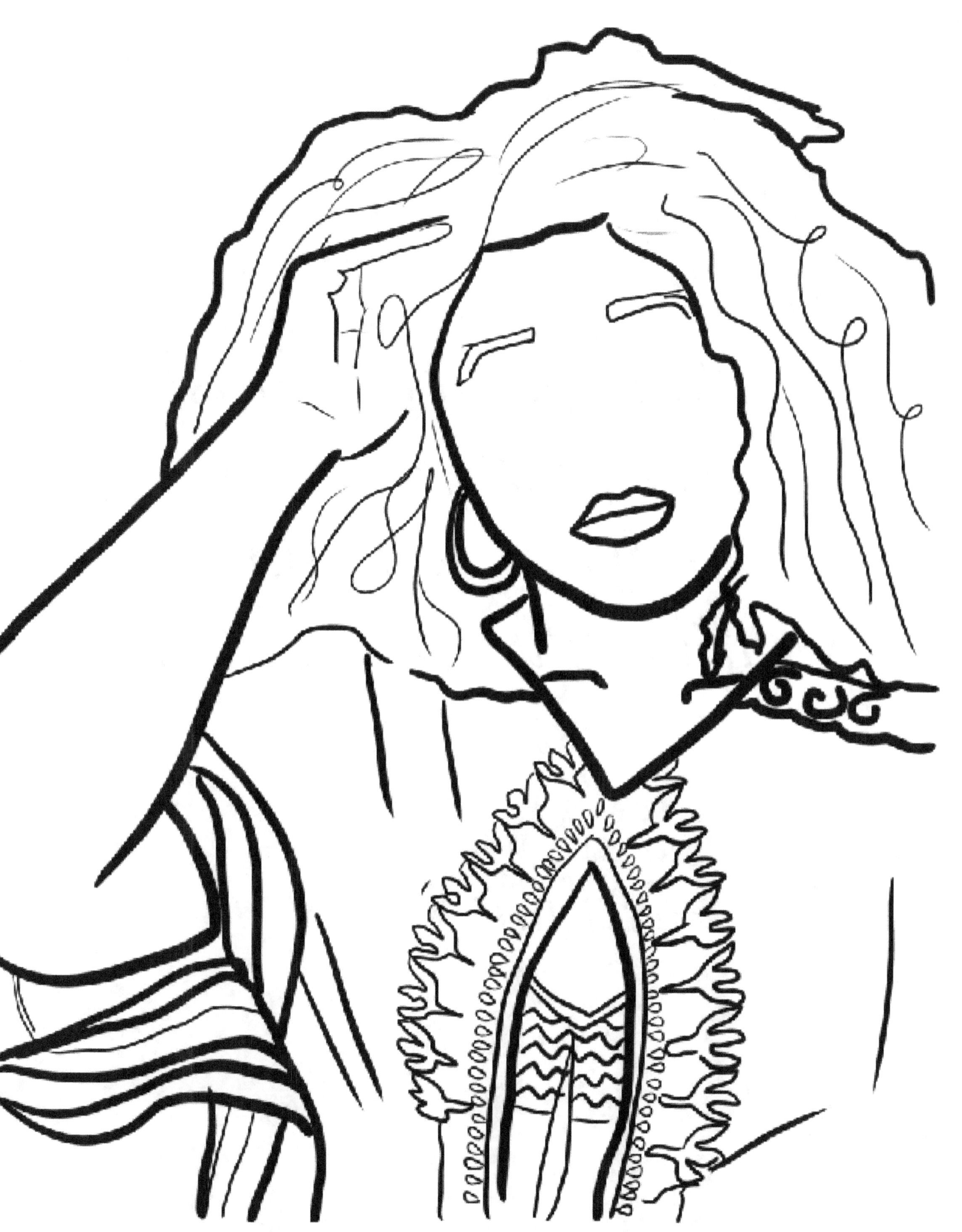

" *You can accomplish ANY goal. Don't let anyone tell you differently. No goal is too out of reach!*"

—Naomi Winston

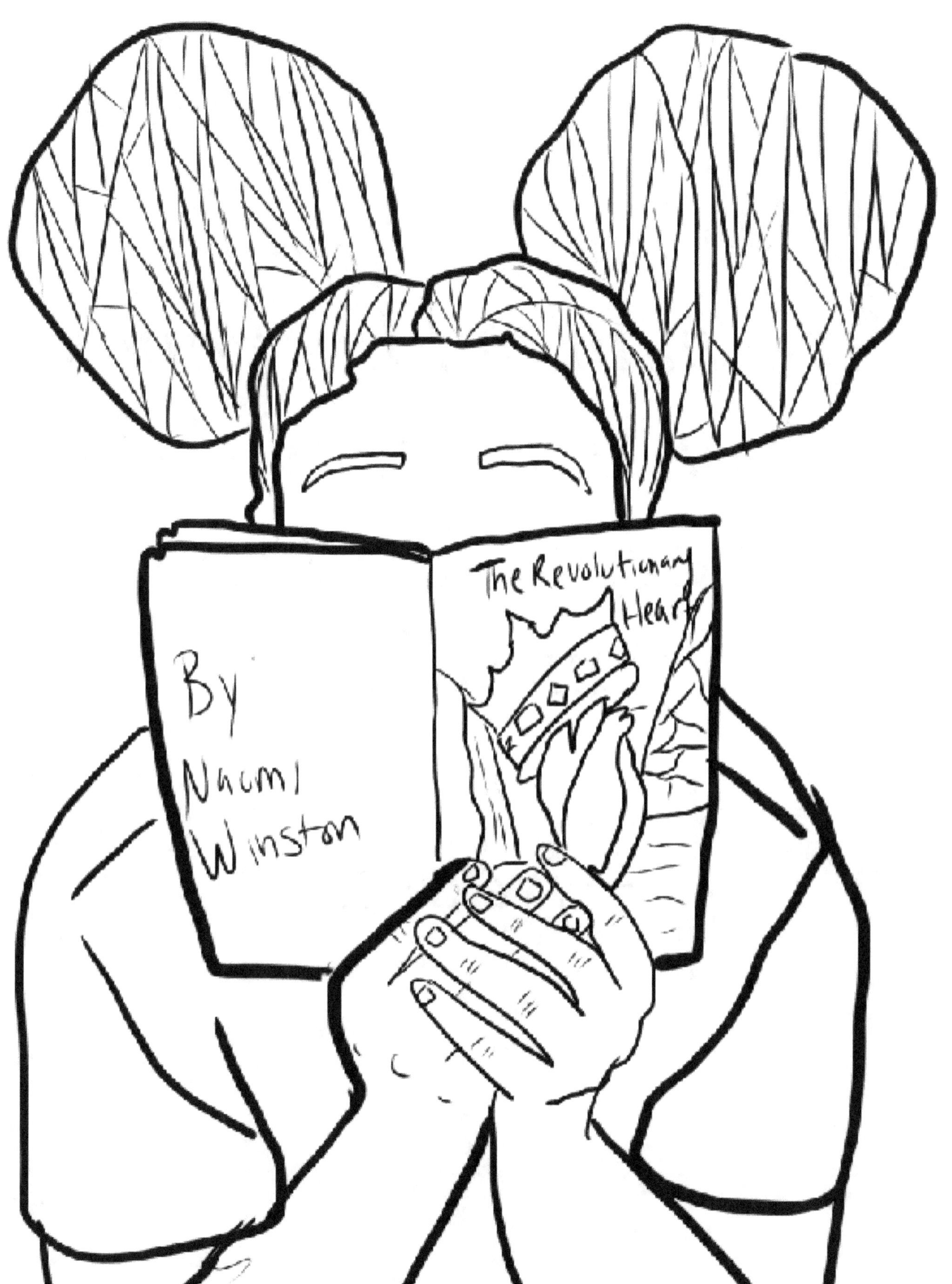
By
Naomi
Winston
The Revolutionary
Heart

"If a man put his hands on you once he will do it again. Protect yourself."

—Naomi

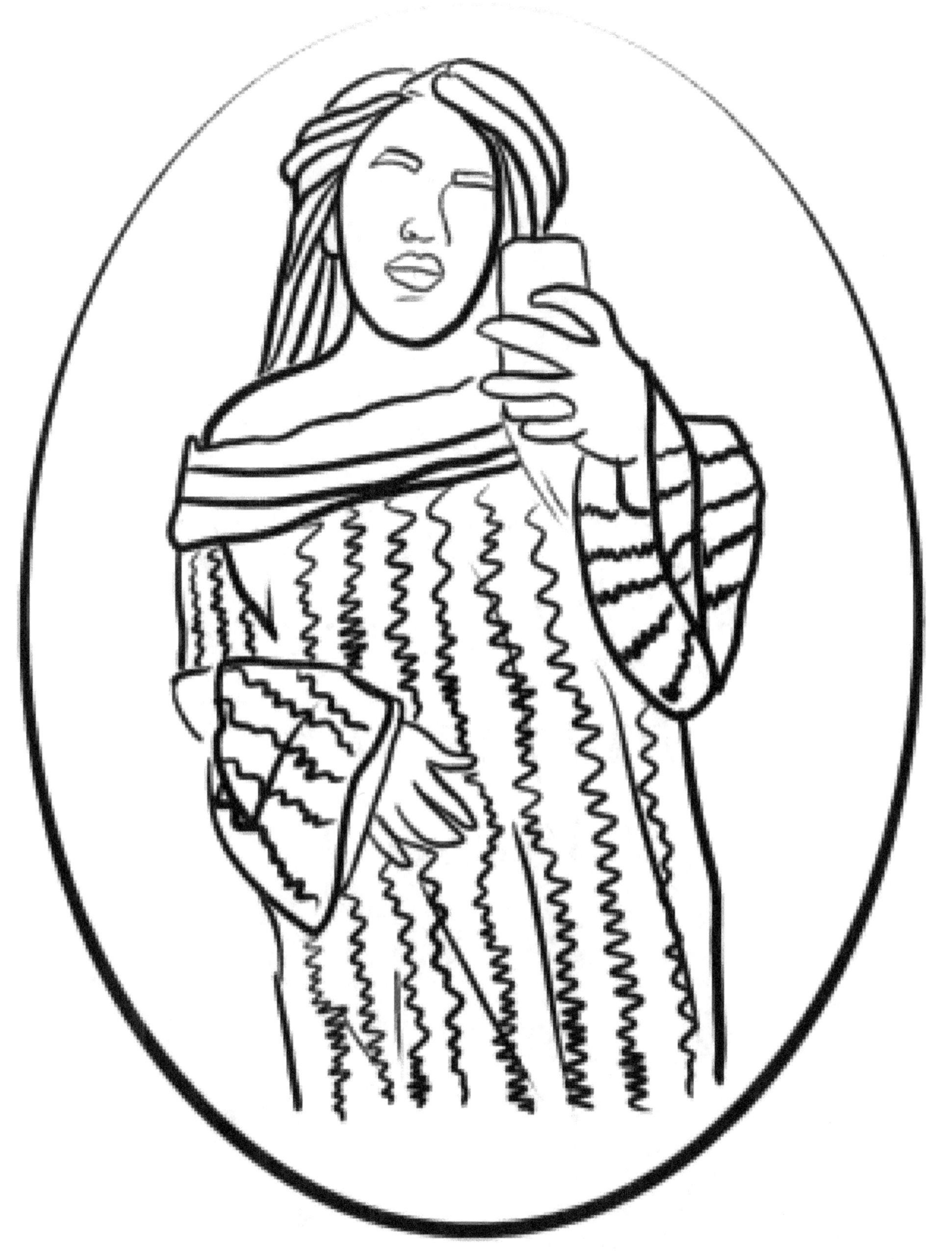

I love my hair, I love my skin, all beauty comes from within.
—Majeanne

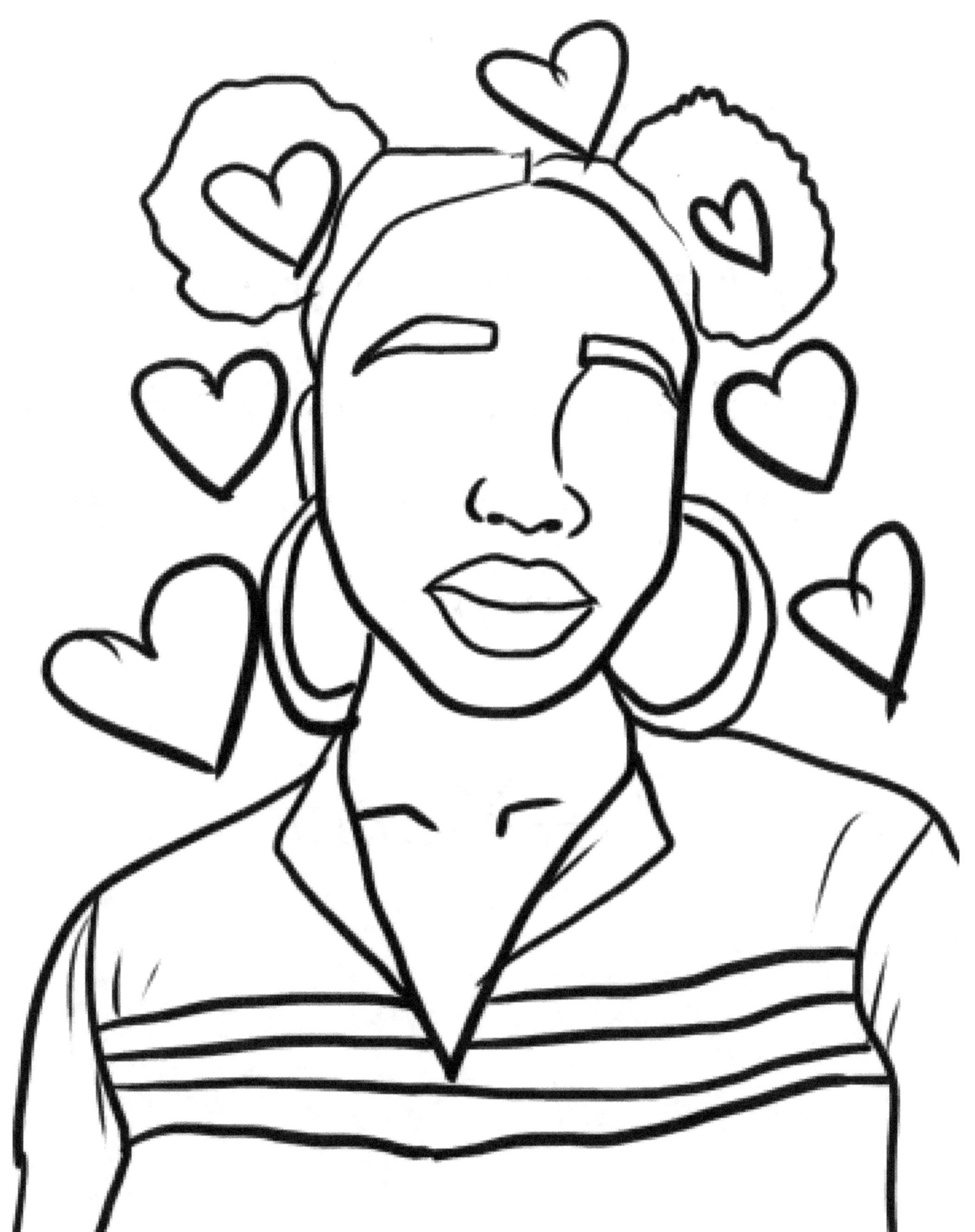

"The world is going to hate you so you have to love yourself twice as hard."

—Naomi

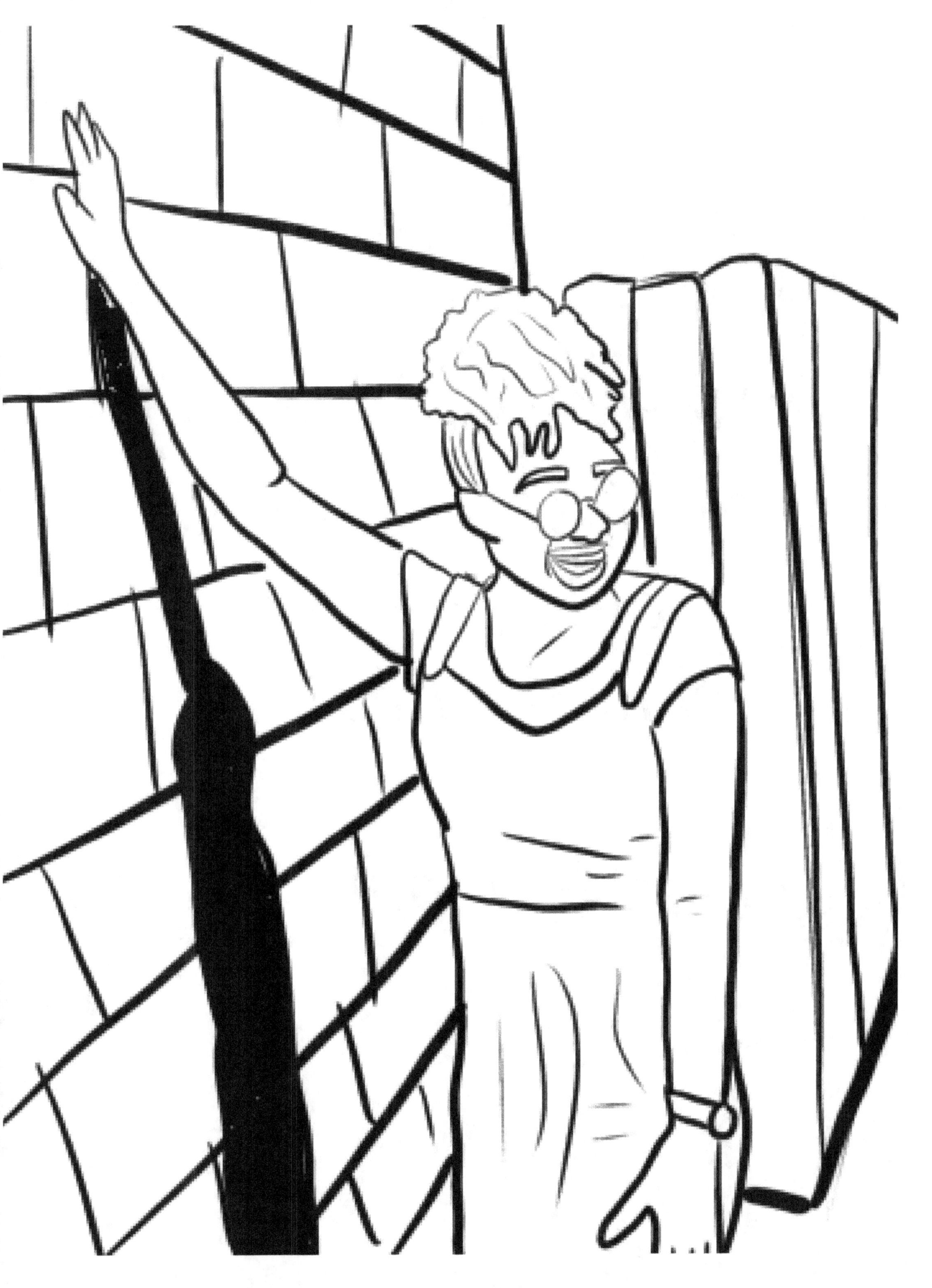

"Don't try to grow up
too fast most of us
would pay to be
children again."

—Naomi

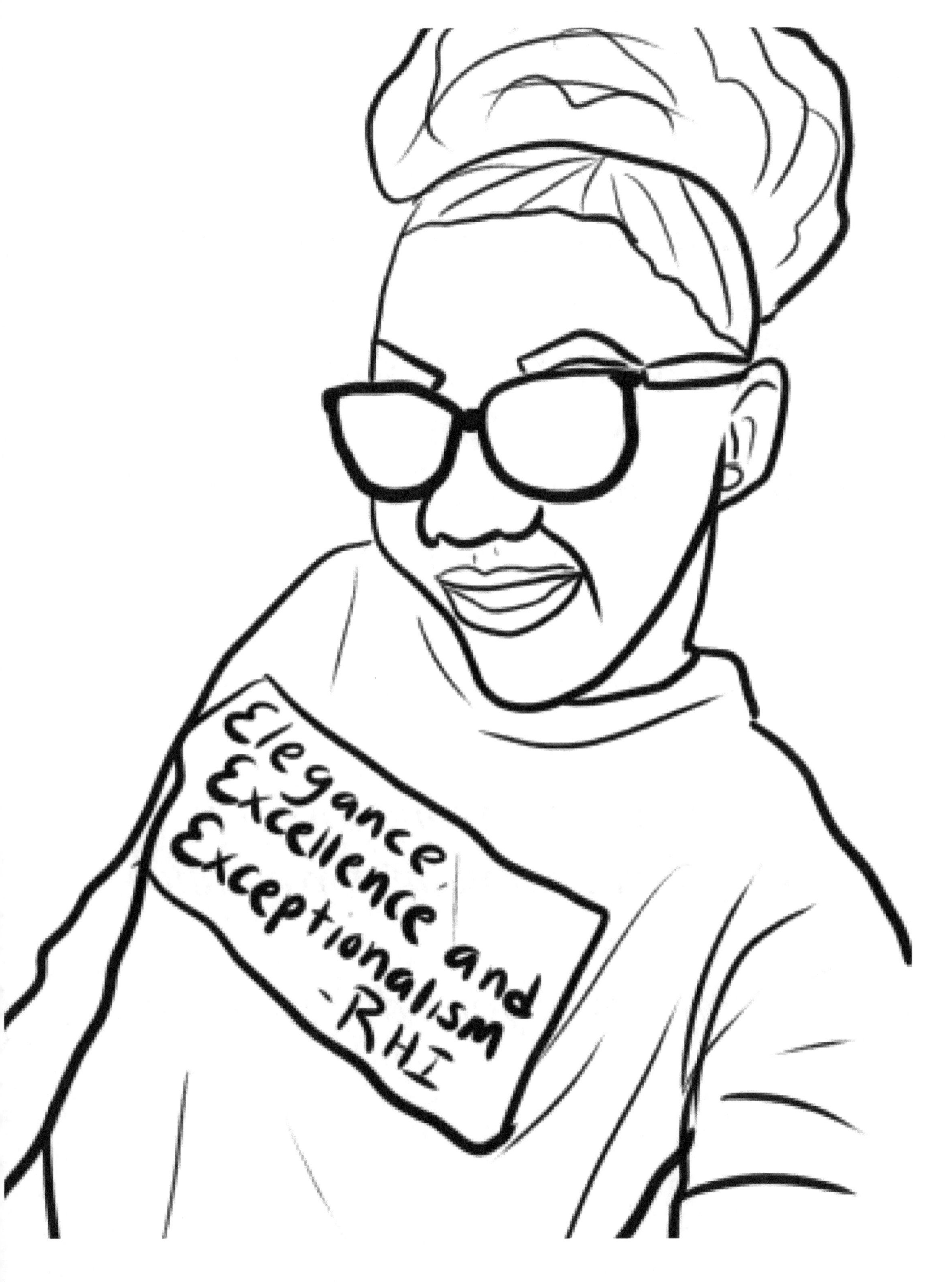

Elegance
Excellence and
Exceptionalism
-RHI

Your name holds power
Your name holds meaning

Your name makes you who you are
Your name is who the world will see you as

You name is important

Don't let anyone forget it
Don't let anyone mispronounce it
Don't let anyone disrespect it

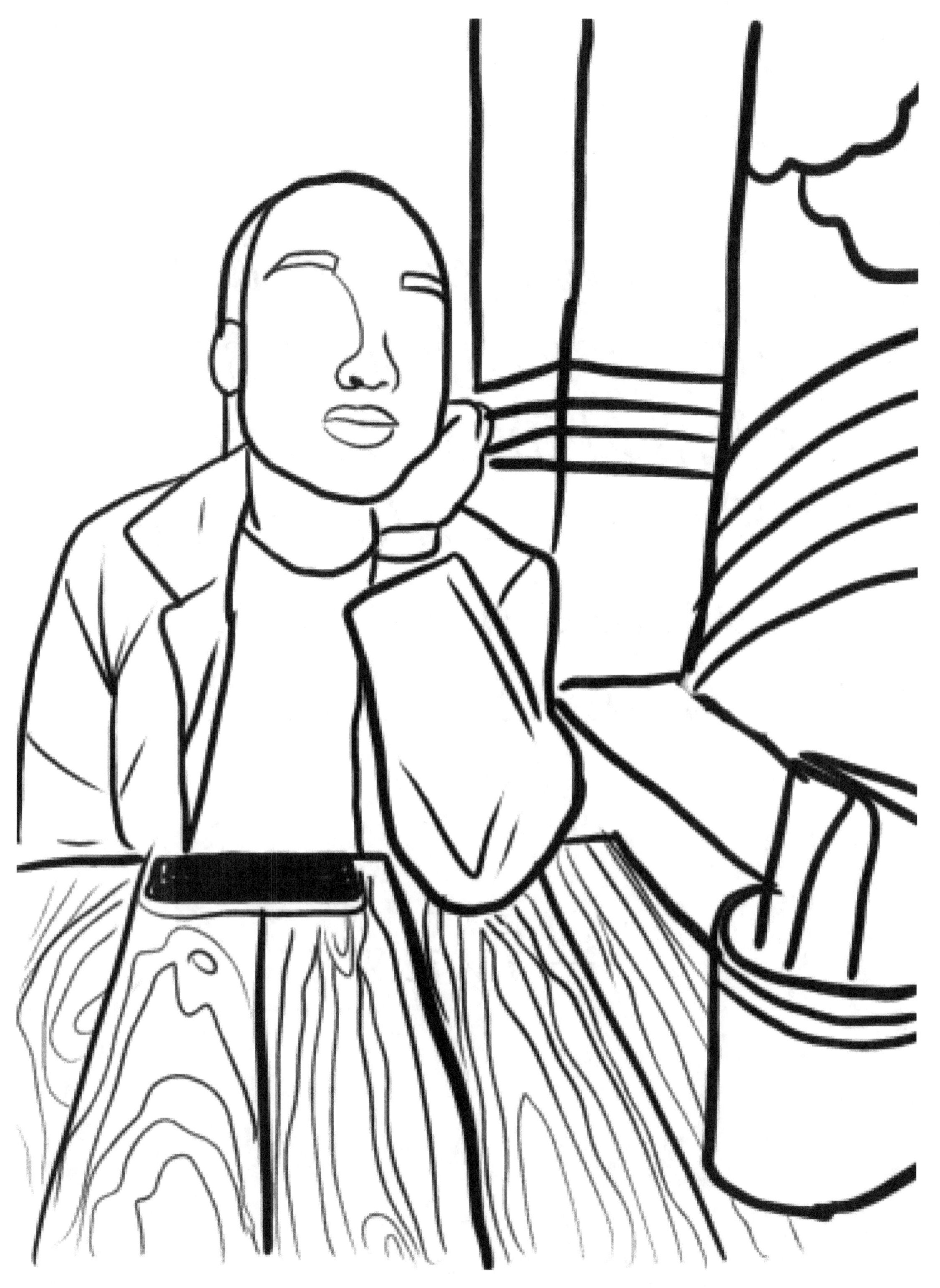

"You are wonderfully and beautifully made, created in God's image. The creator loves you unconditionally, and that will NEVER change."

—*Tynesia*

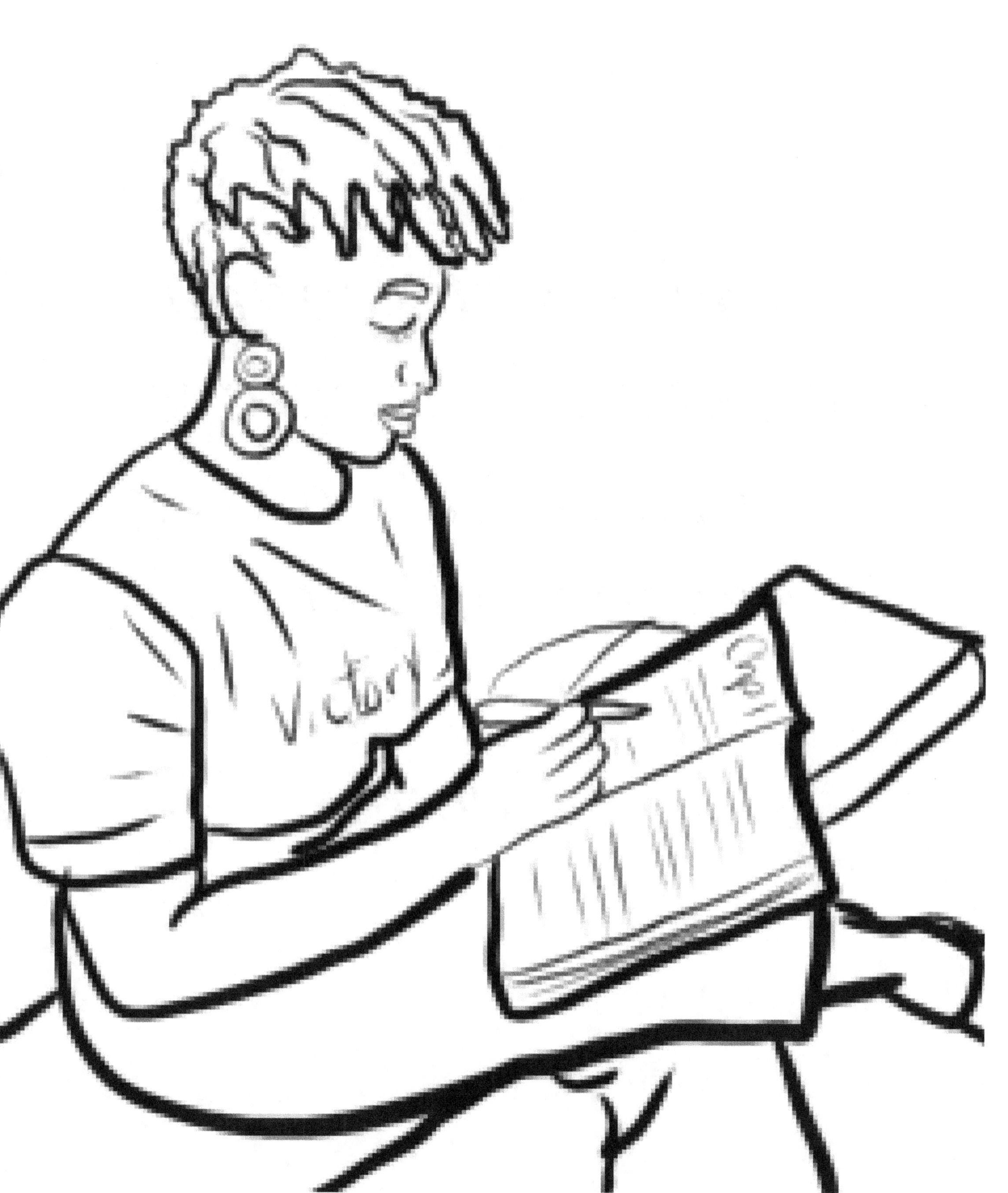

Victory

"There is strength in numbers but there is resilience in knowing when to walk alone."

—Naomi

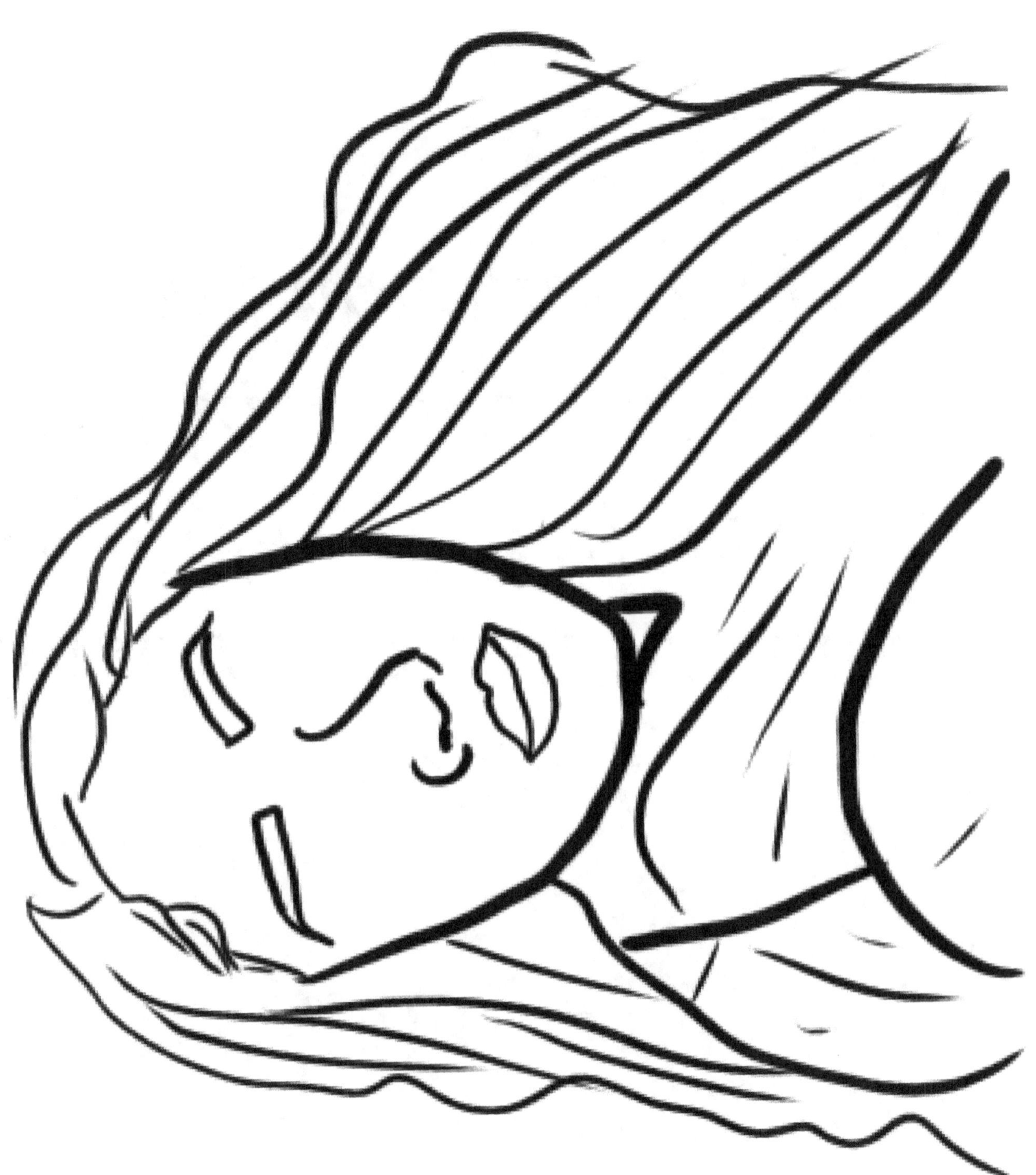

"The pain you feel is real and the pain you feel matters. Don't hide yourself in fear of being judged."

—Naomi

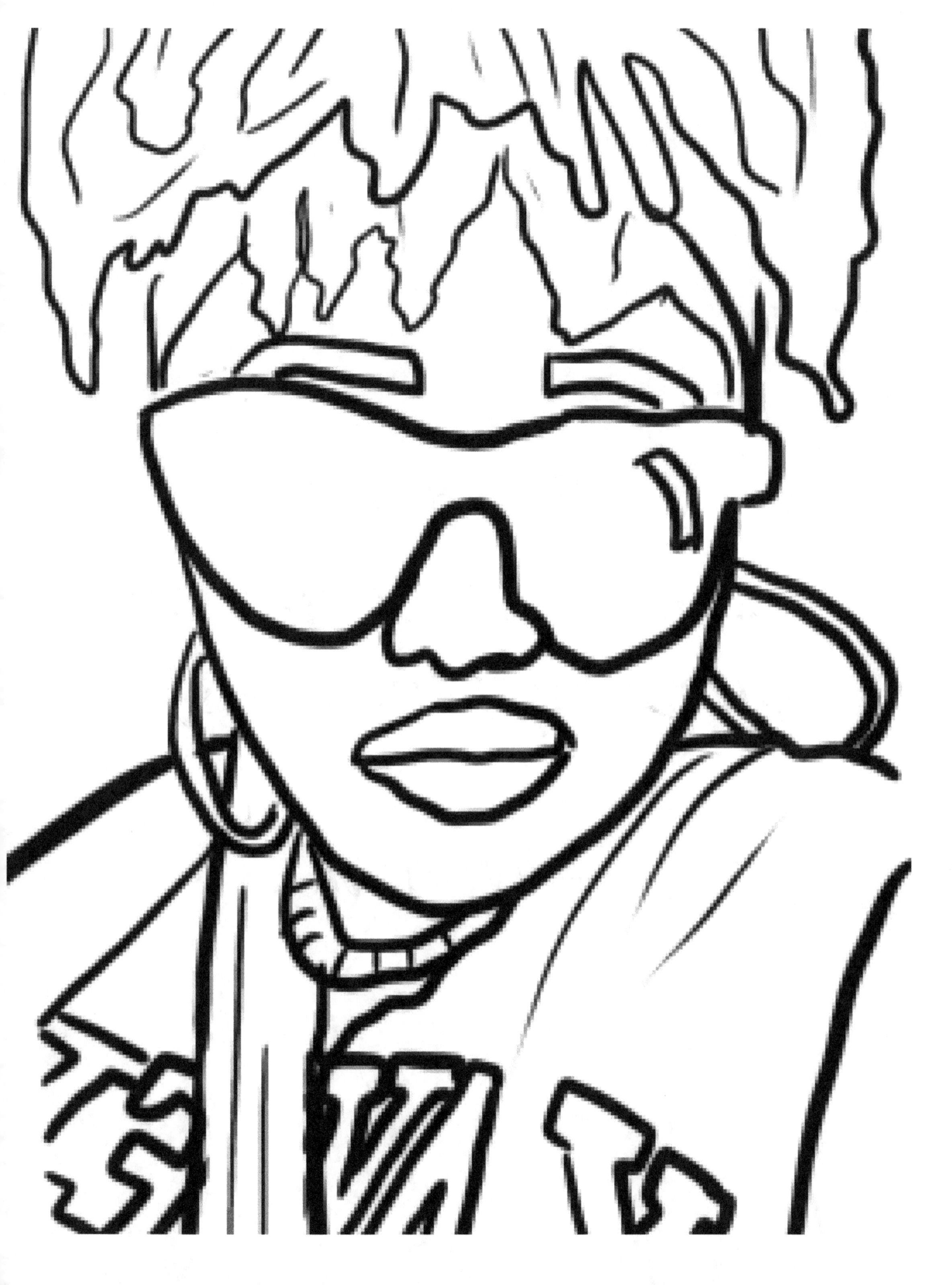

"It's hard to be a beautiful black girl but you make it look easy."

—Naomi

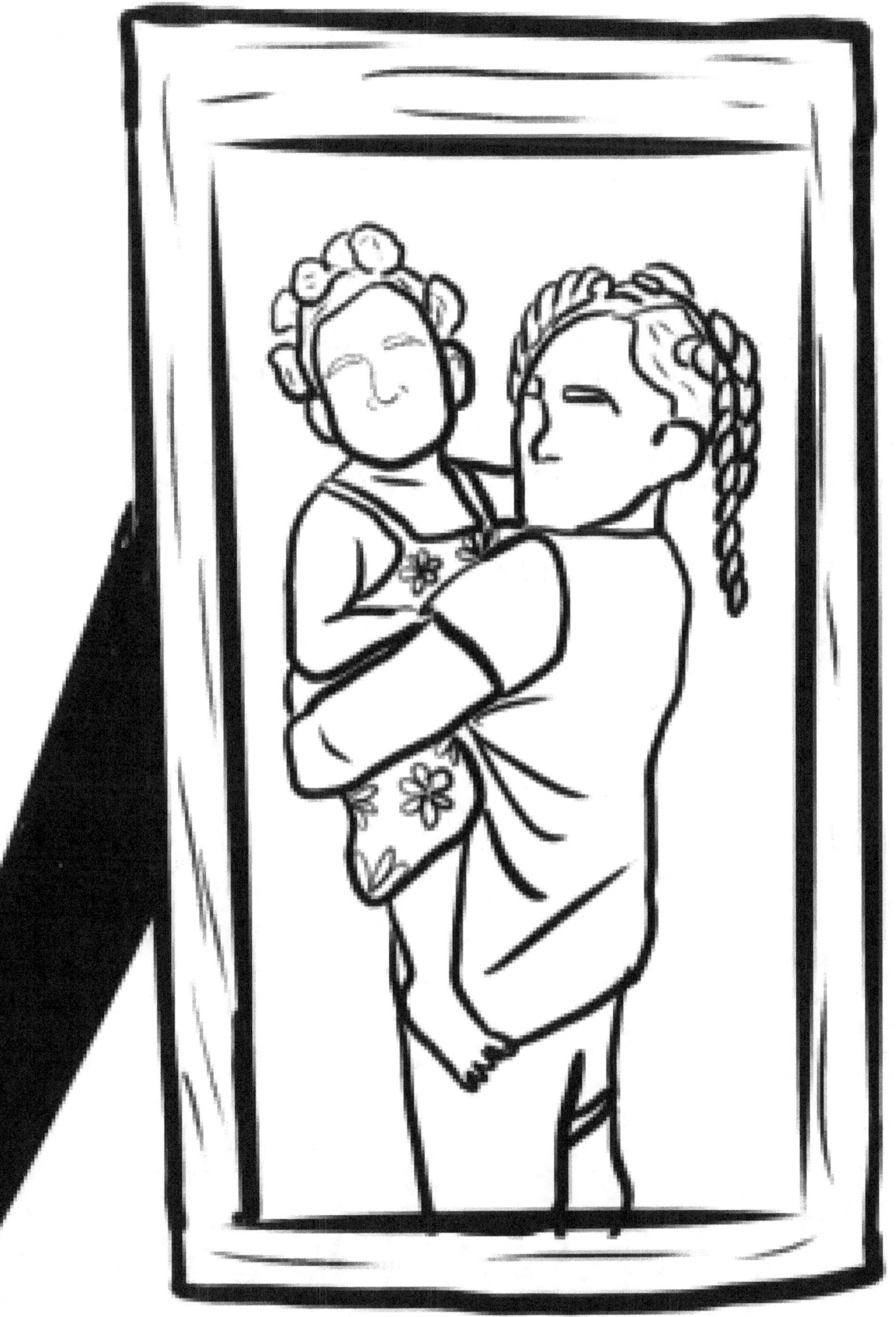

"Work hard but don't let your work destroy you."

—Naomi

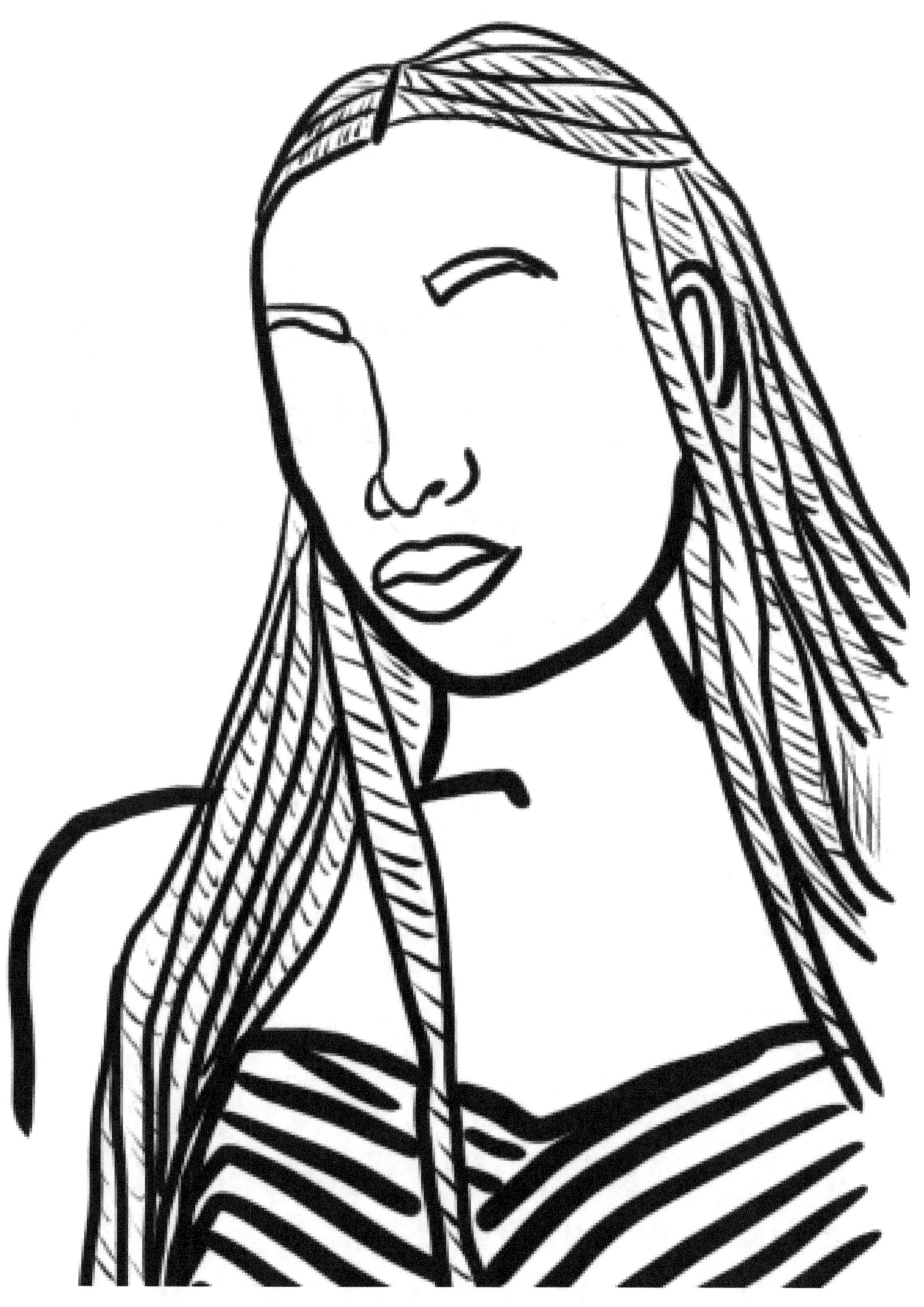

"Not everyone is going
to love you but don't let
that keep you from
being loving."

—Naomi

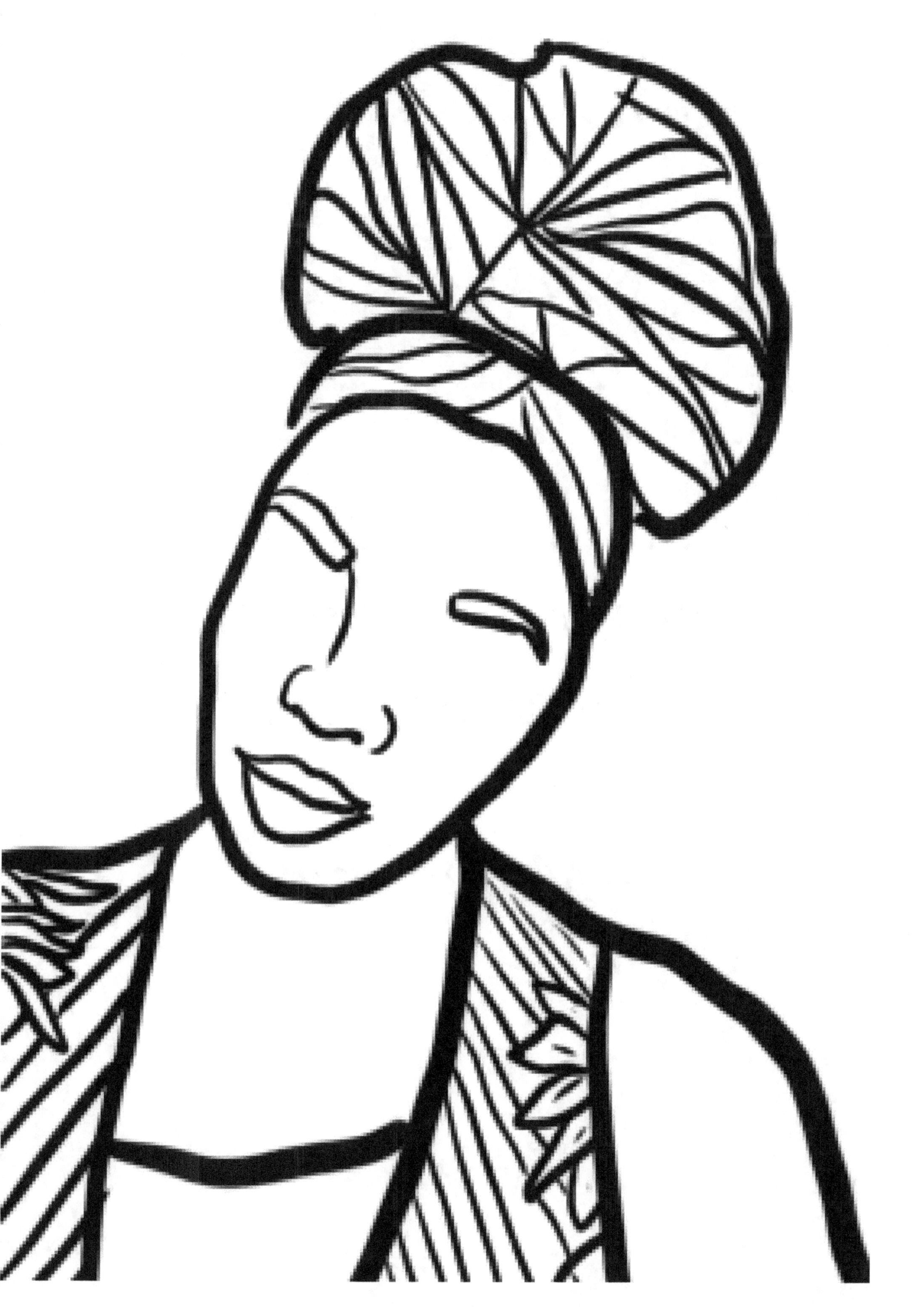

For all the pretty black babies that are gonna color your book

—Majeanne

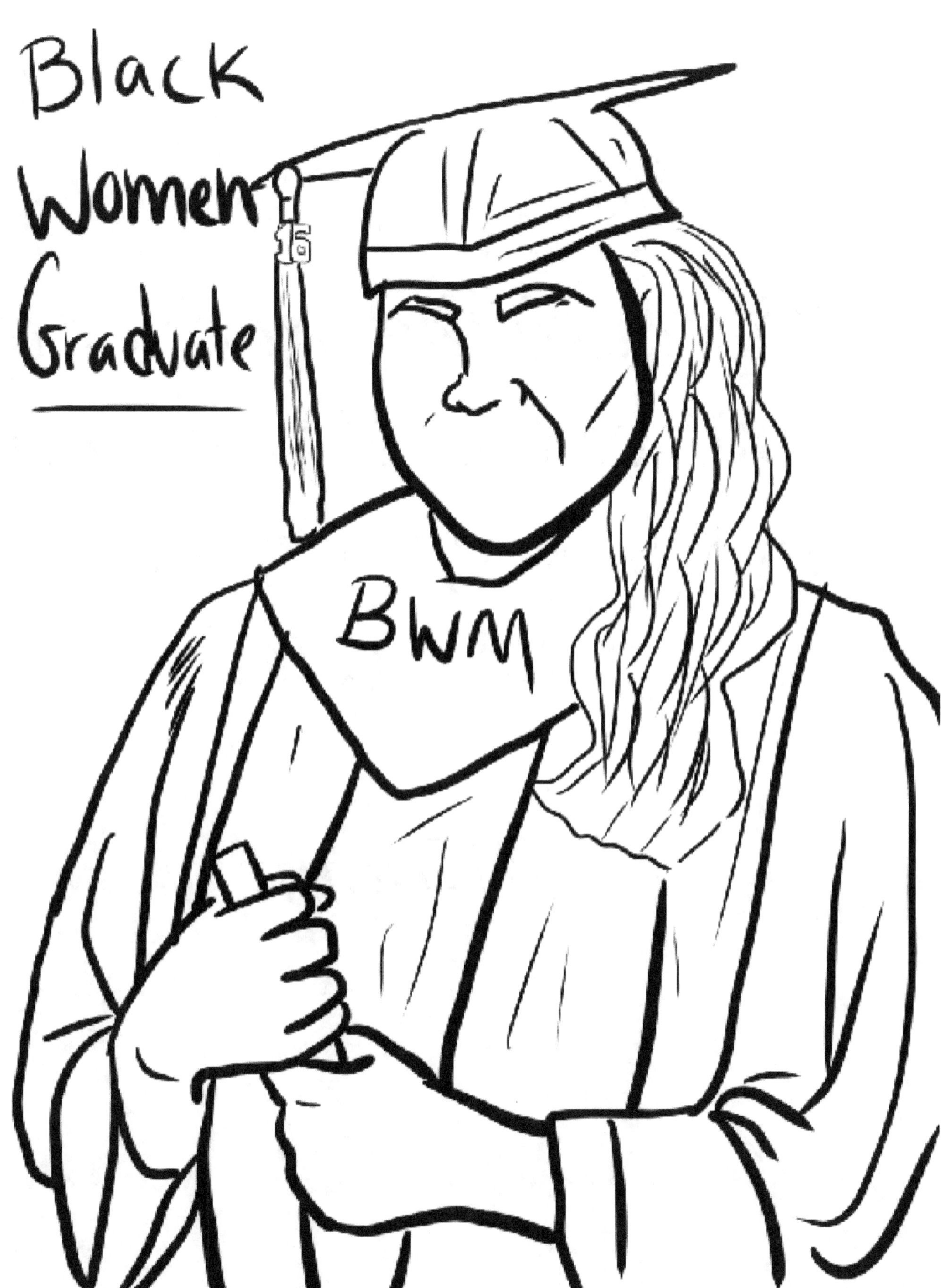

Black
Women
Graduate
BWM

"You are the product of your circle. If you want to win keep winners in your circle."

—Naomi

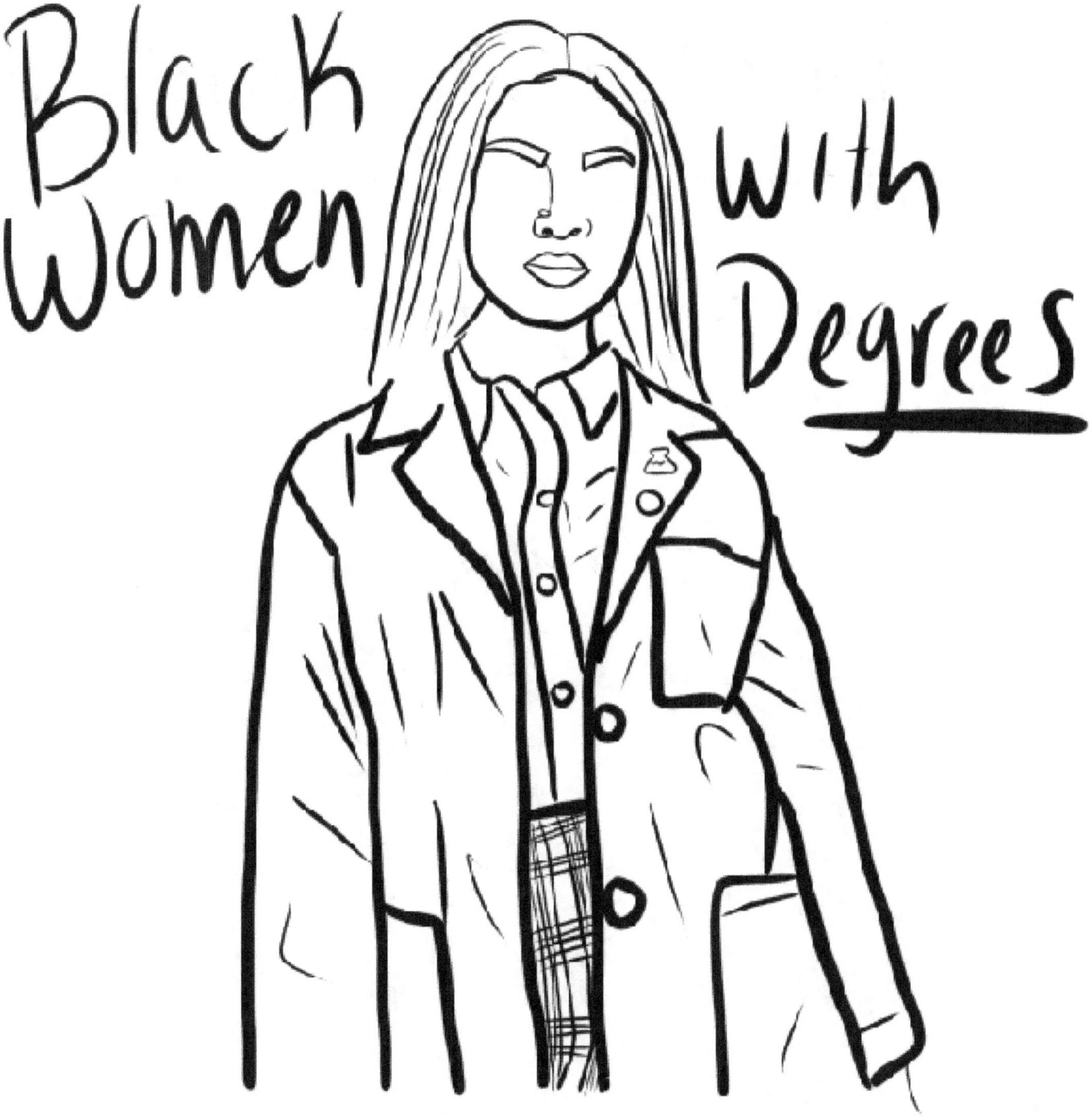

Black
Women
with
Degrees

"*Don't let the world silence you. Be loud and be proud.*"

—*Naomi*

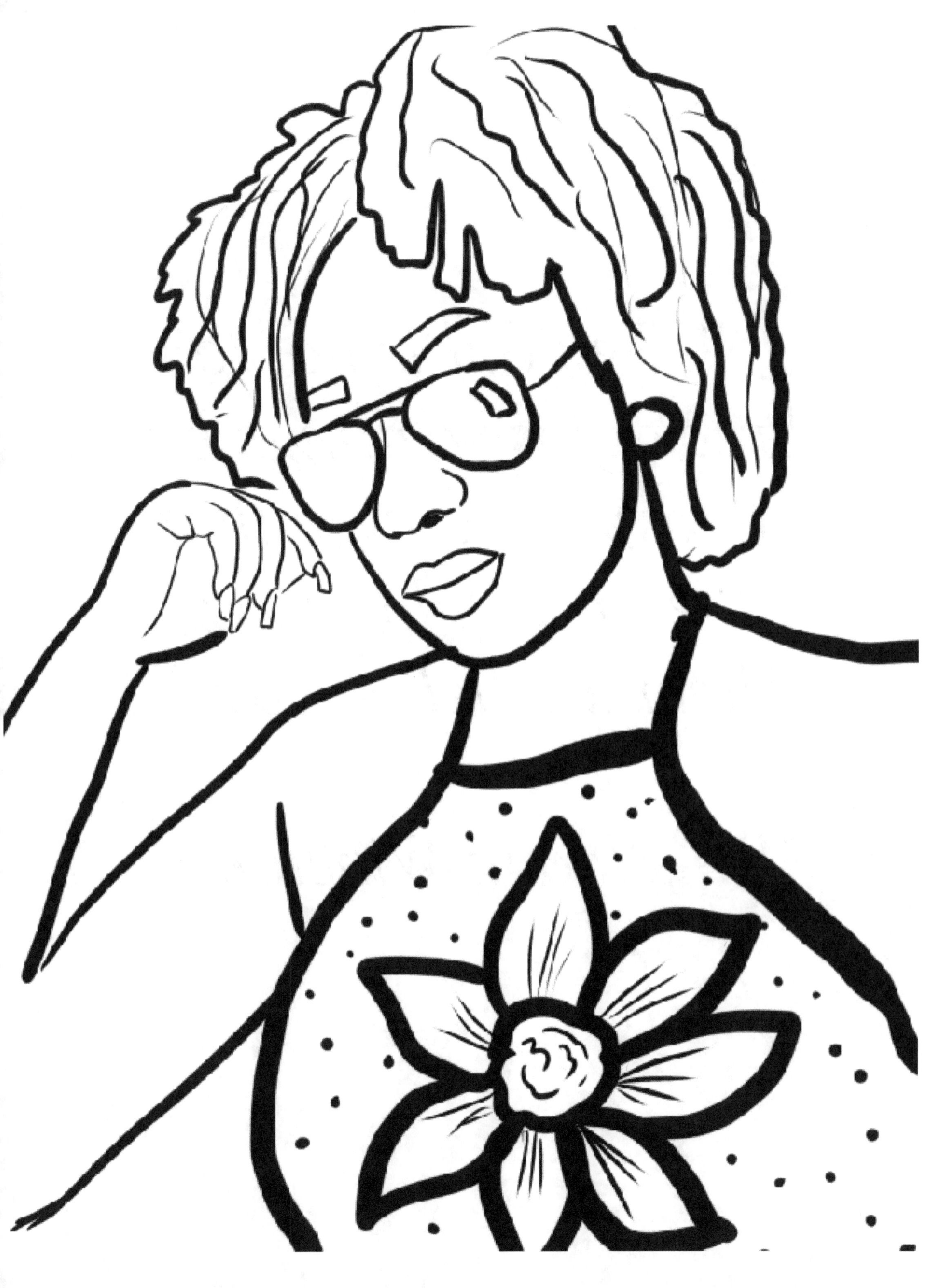

"The goal is not to
break glass ceilings but
to aspire so high that
the idea of breaking
them are below you."

—Naomi Winston

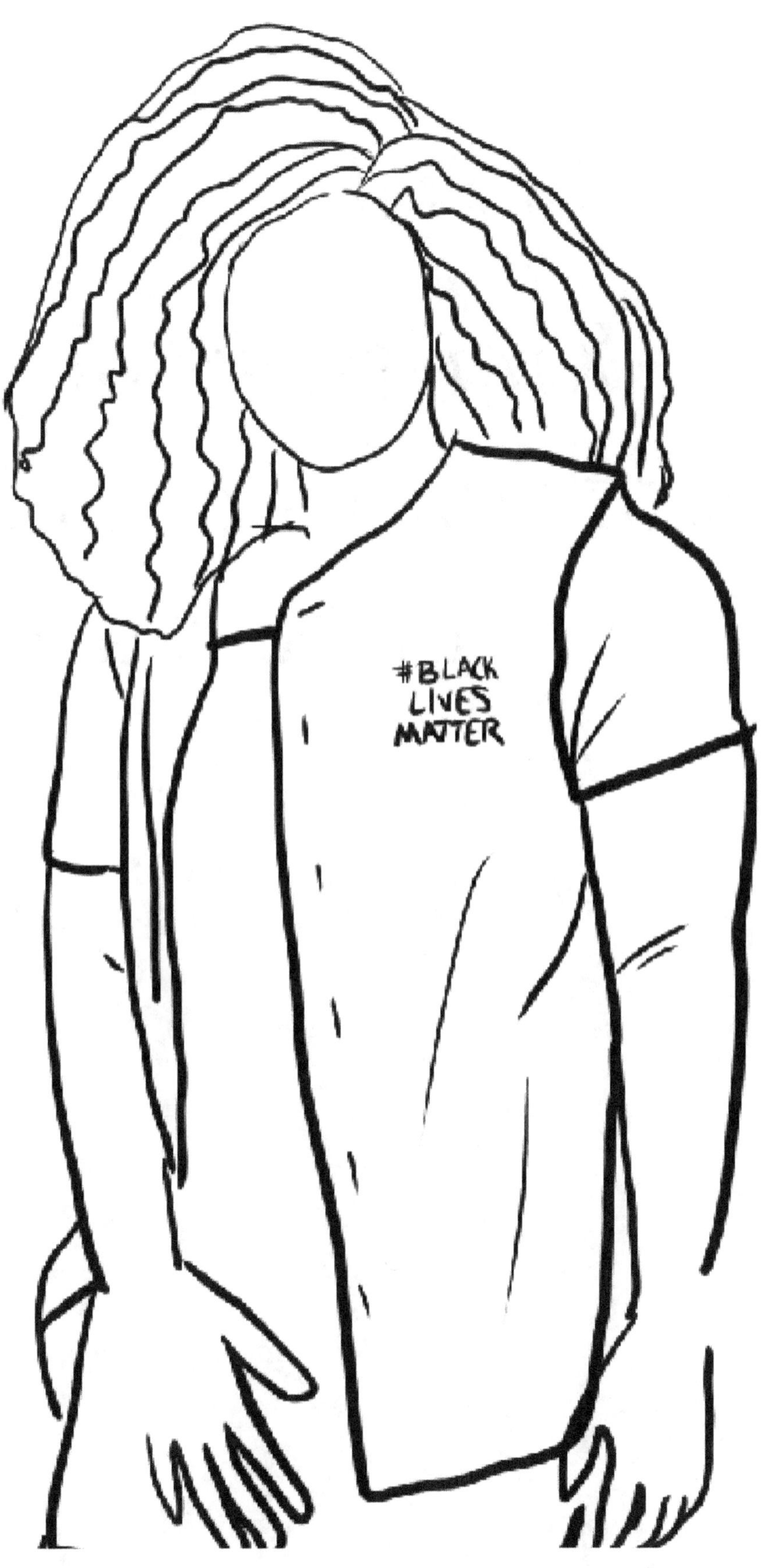

#BLACK
LIVES
MATTER

"Your tears do not
make you weak.It's okay
to not be okay."

—Naomi Winston

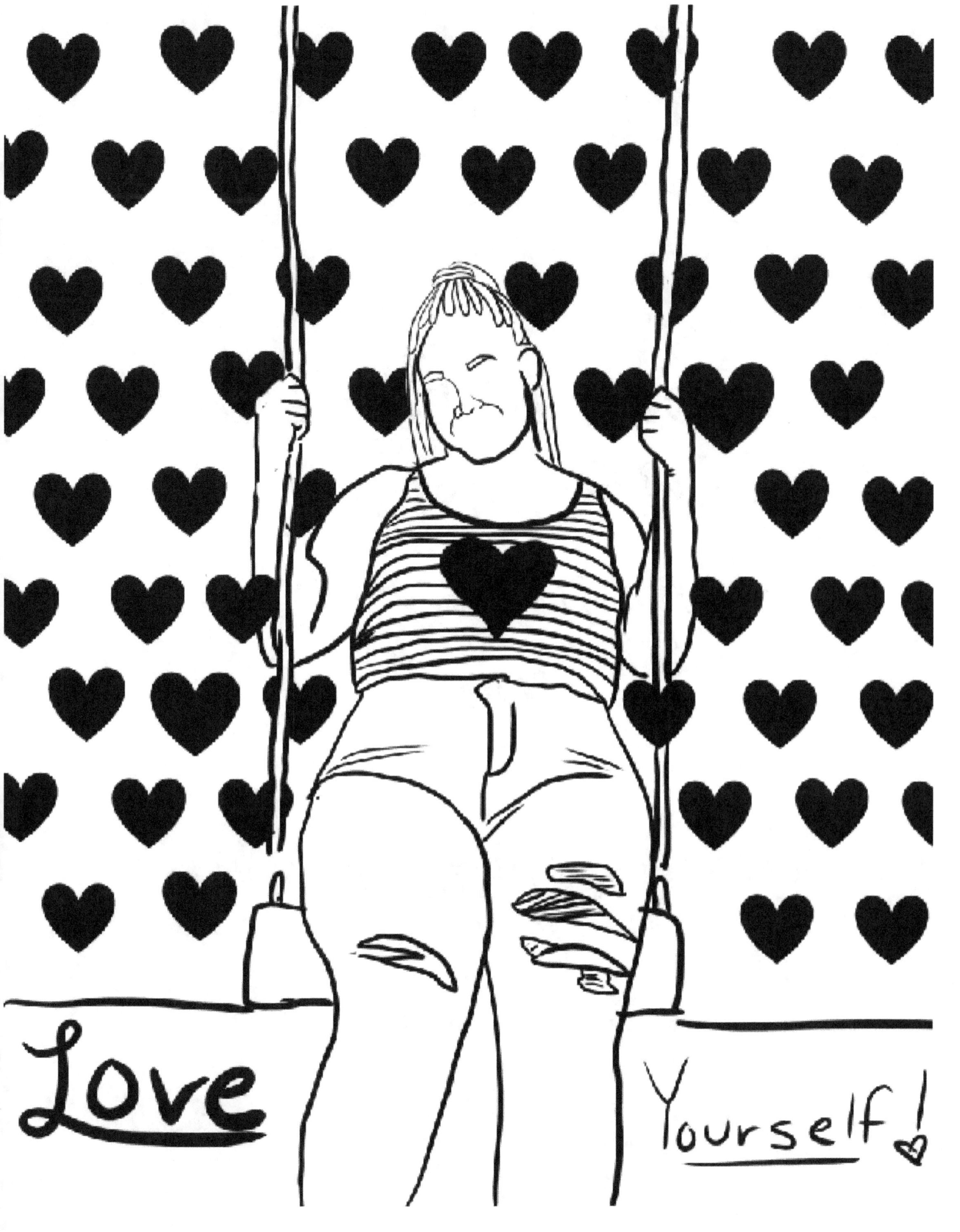

Love
Yourself!

"*You will battle the world constantly so don't fight yourself too.*"

—*Naomi*

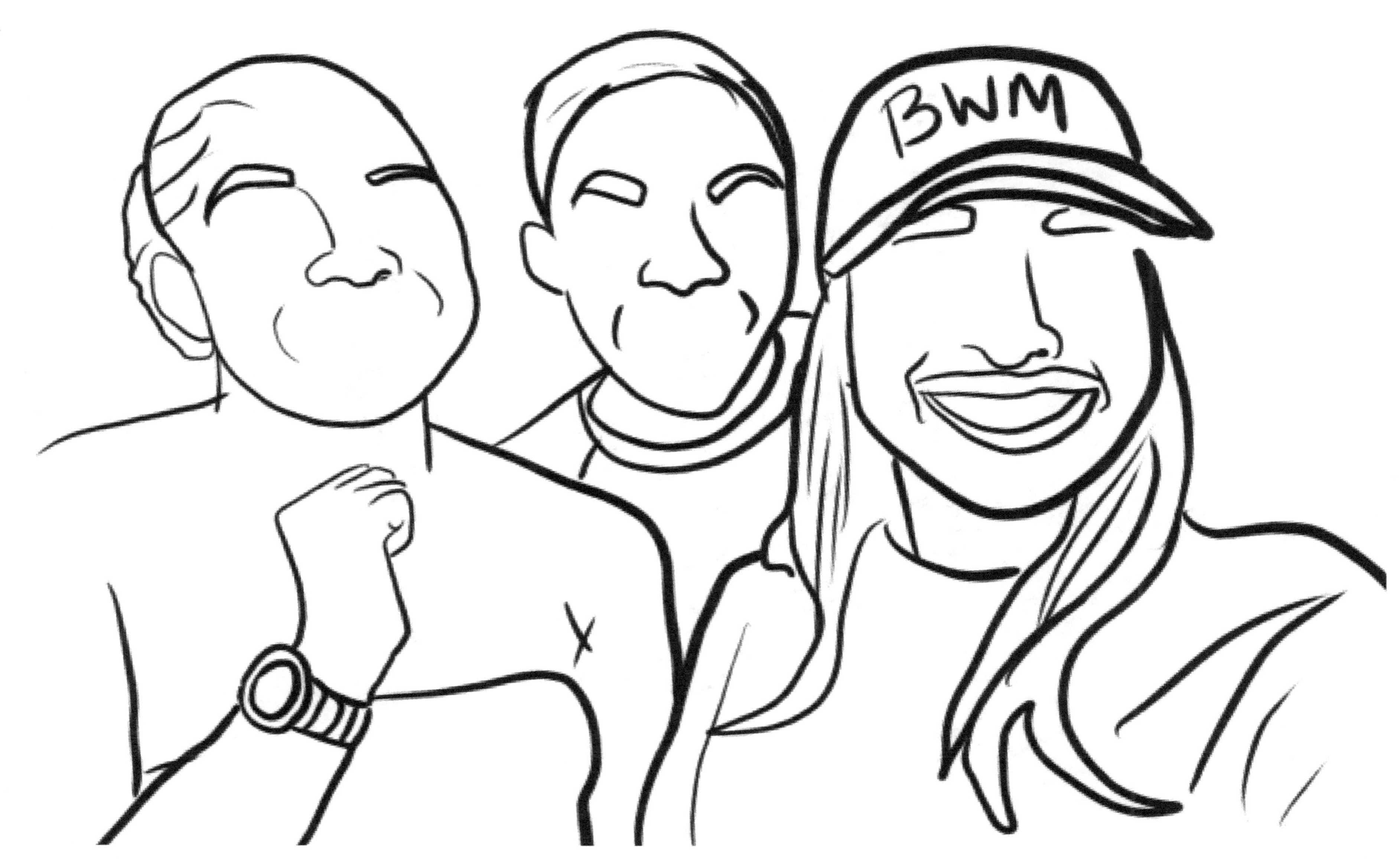

BWM

"You are your ancestors' wildest dreams, go forth and prosper."

—Sydney

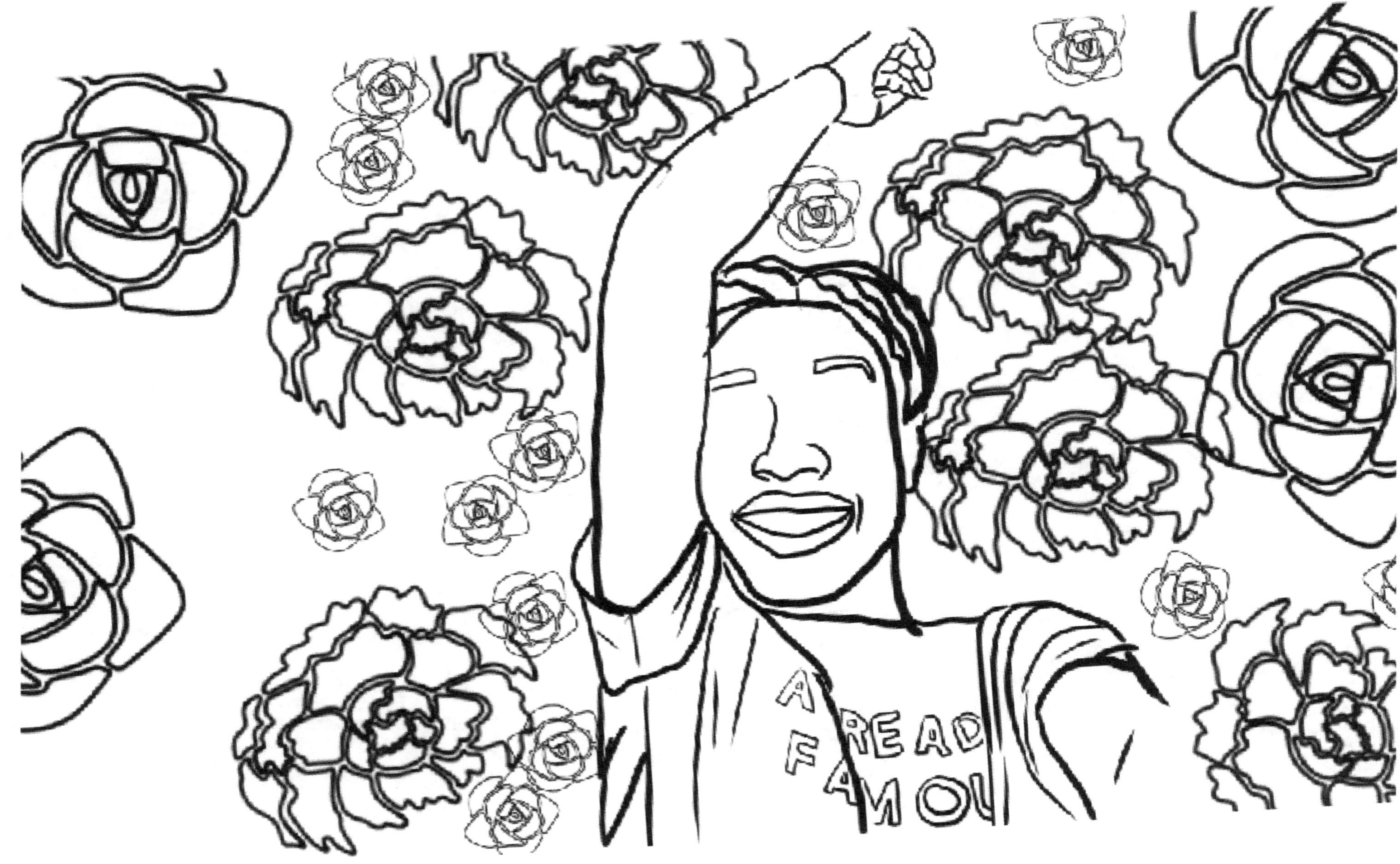
A RE AD
FAMOU

"Let your imagination run free."

—Monet

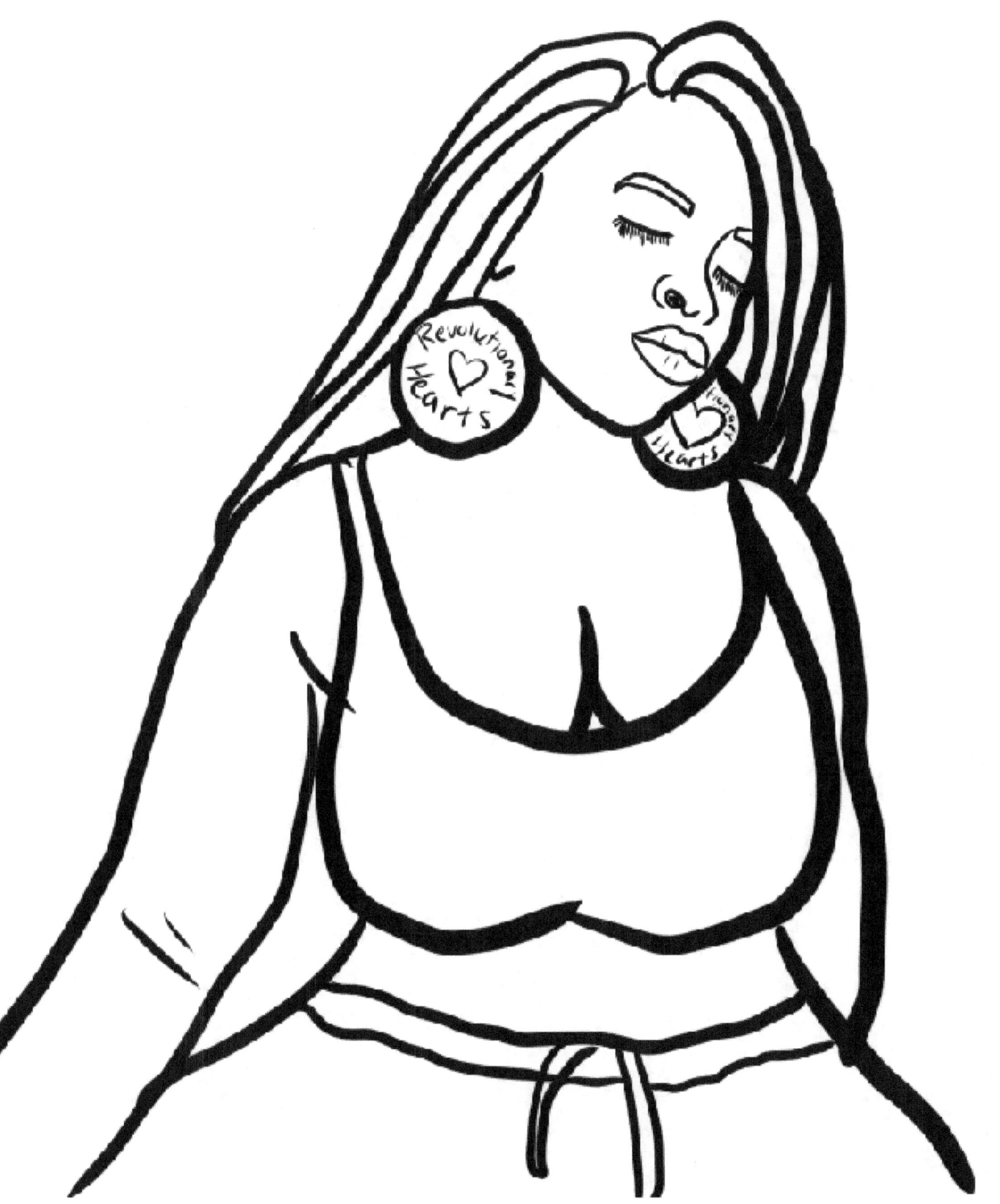

Revolutionary Hearts
Revolutionary Hearts

"Don't let anyone dim
your light."

—Monet

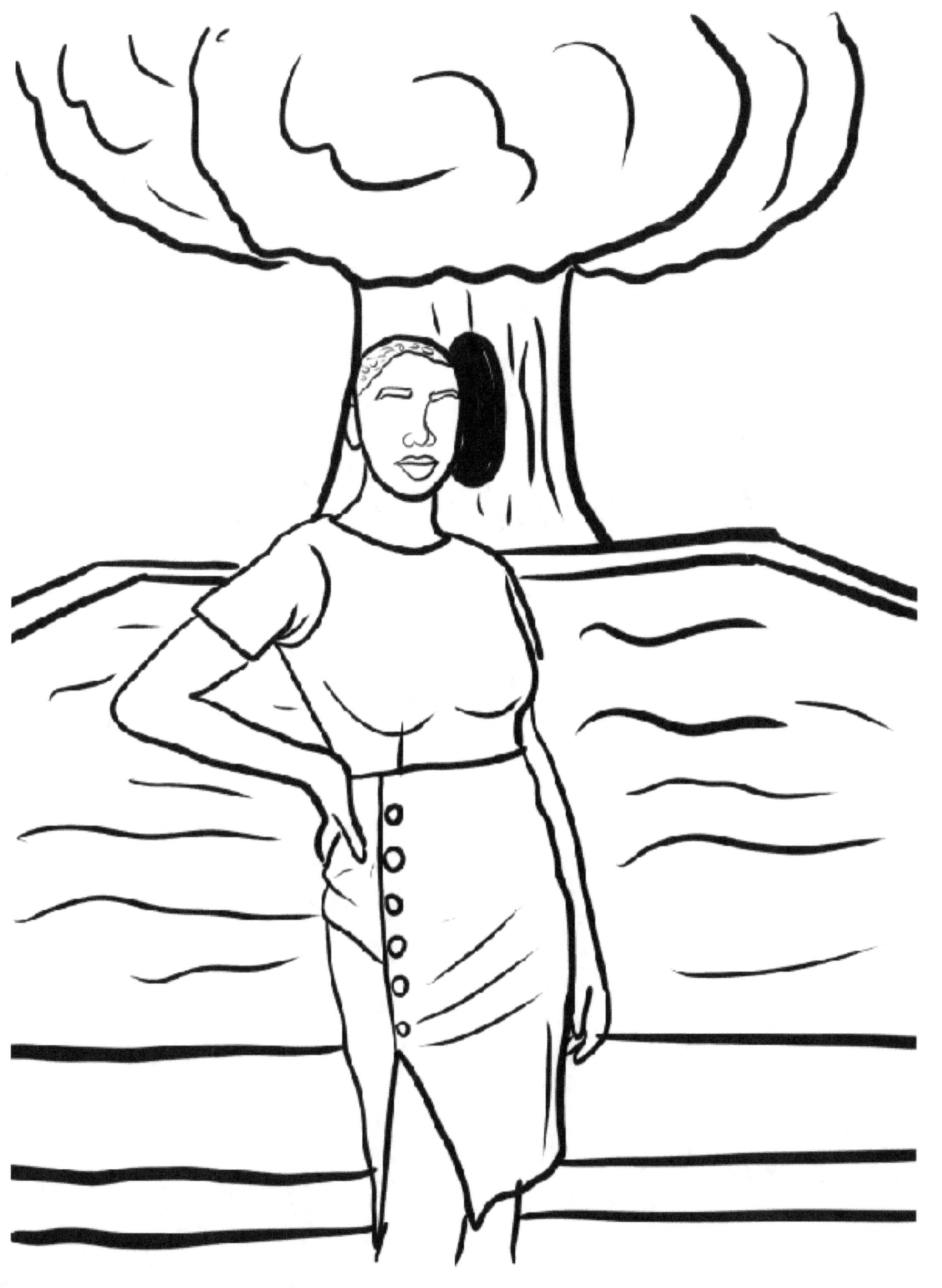

"*Do what you love.*"

—*Monet*

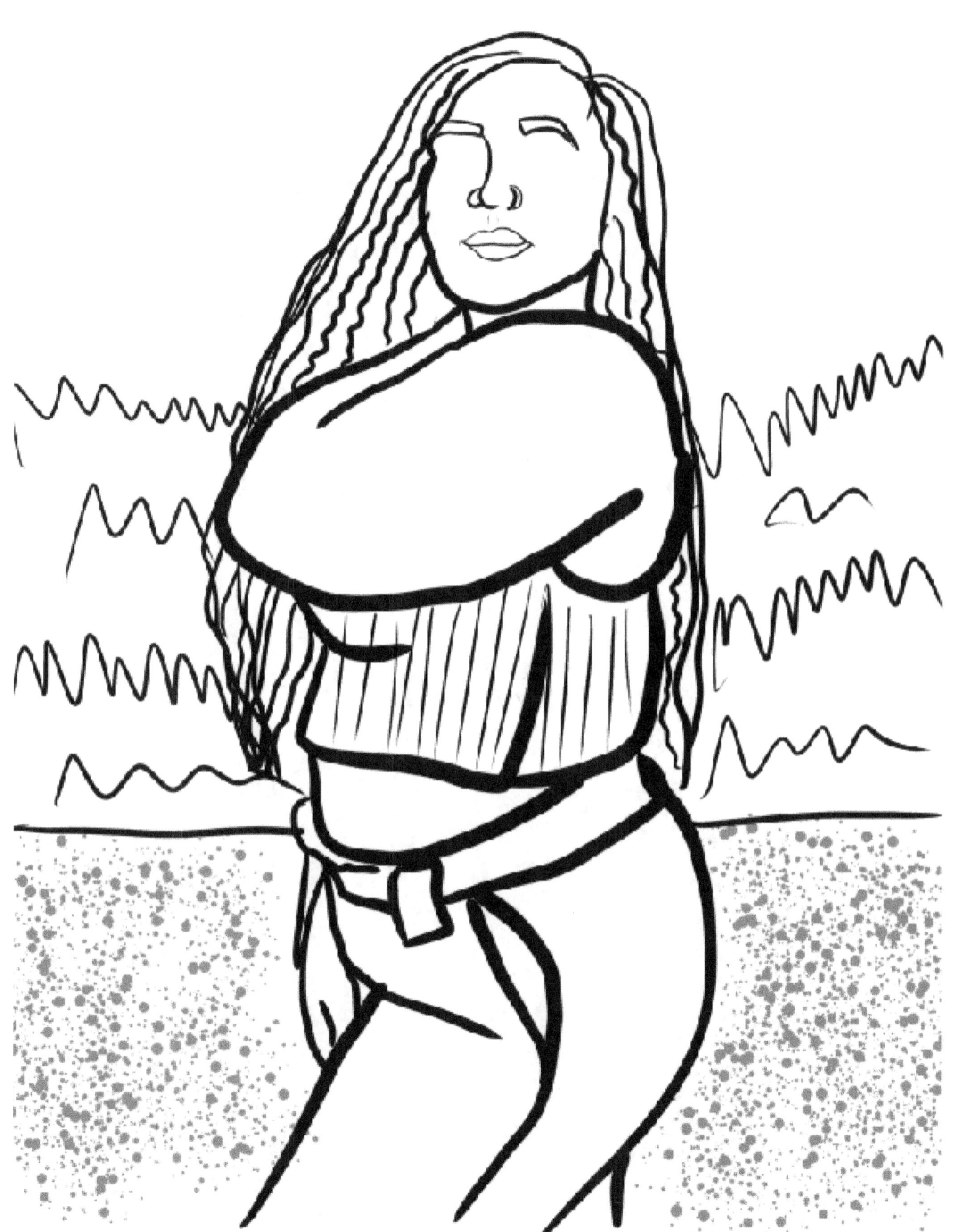

"*Impress yourself first.*"

—Monet

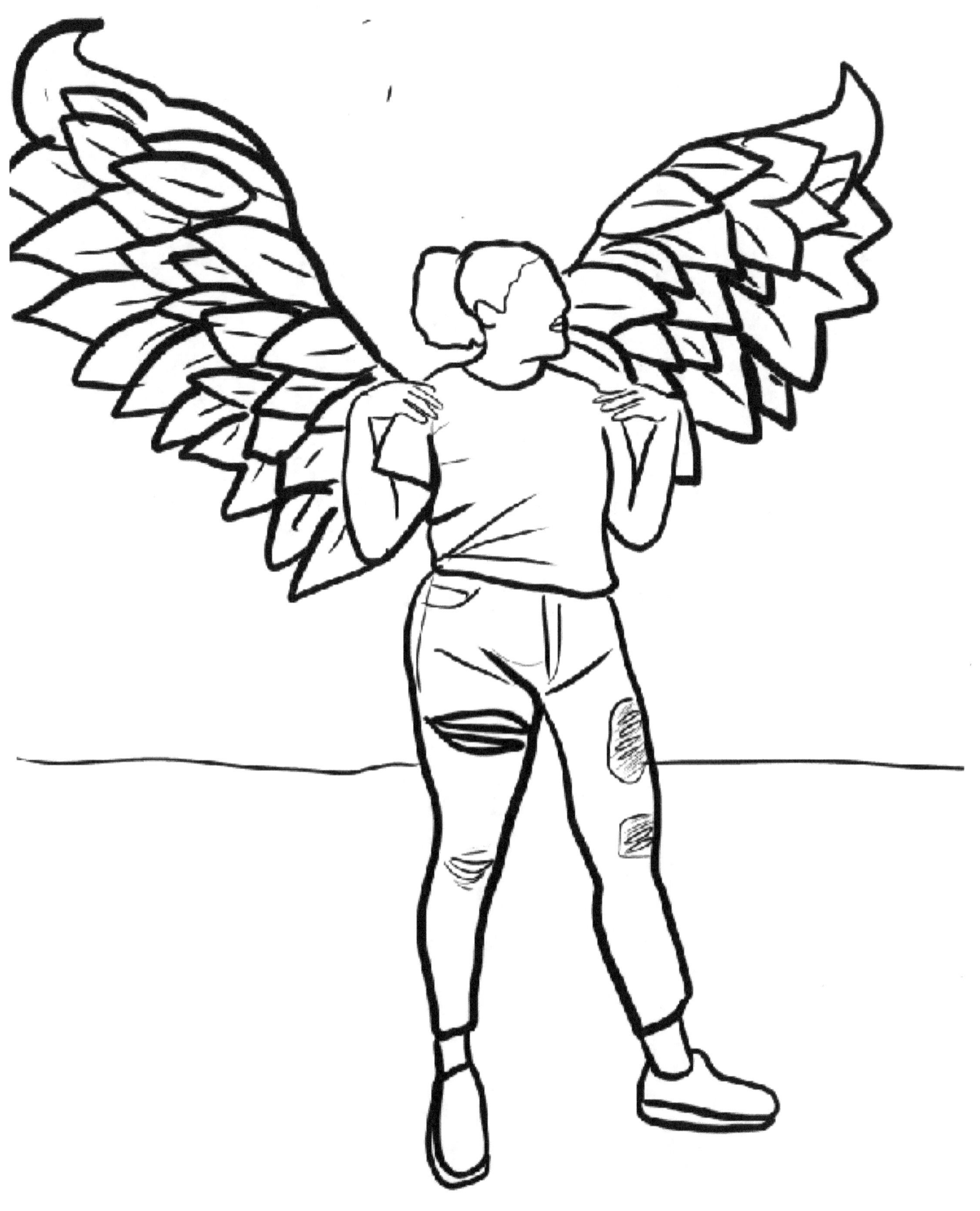

"*Be the hero of your own story.*"

—*Monet*

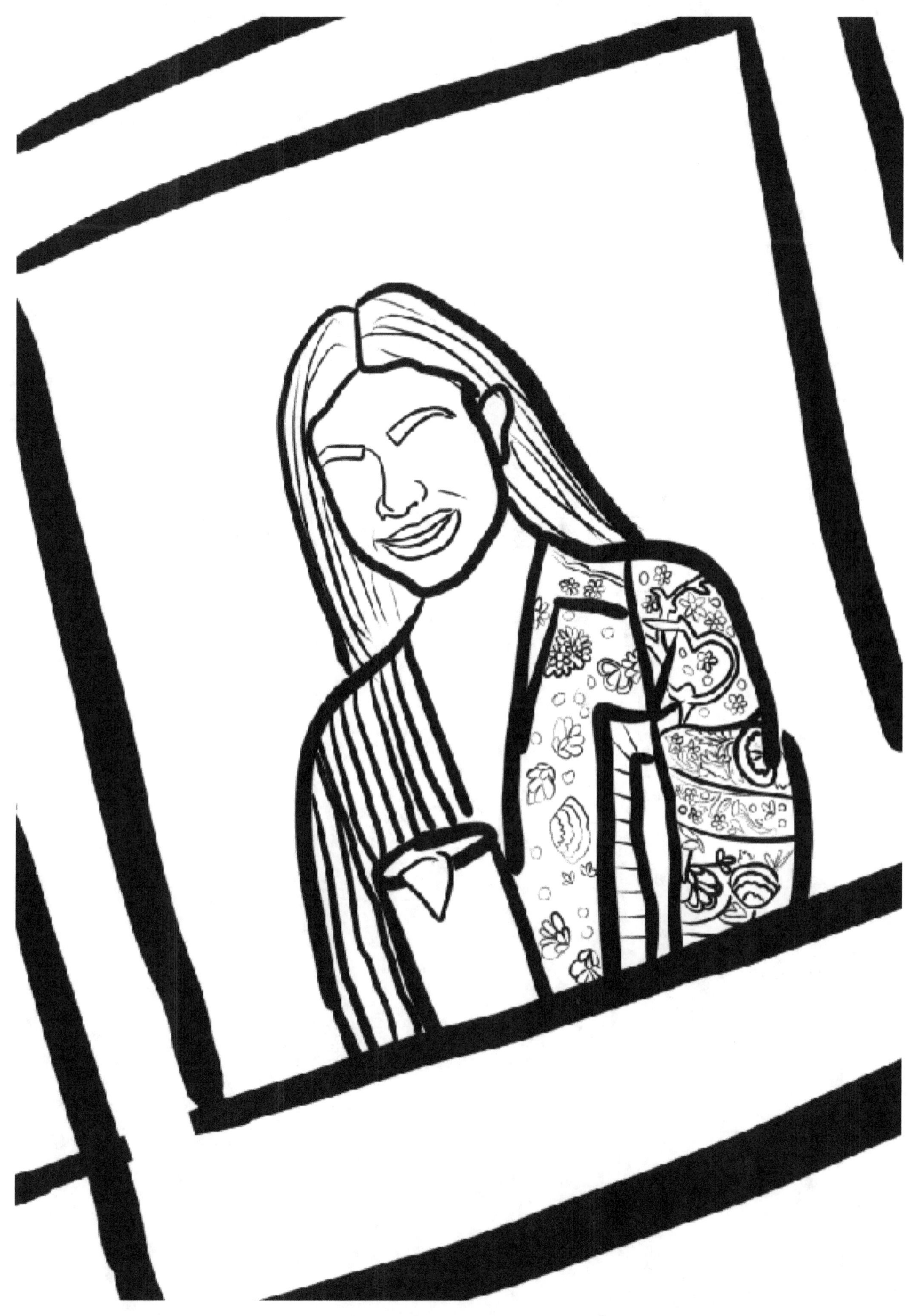

"Create your own
Happiness."

—Monet

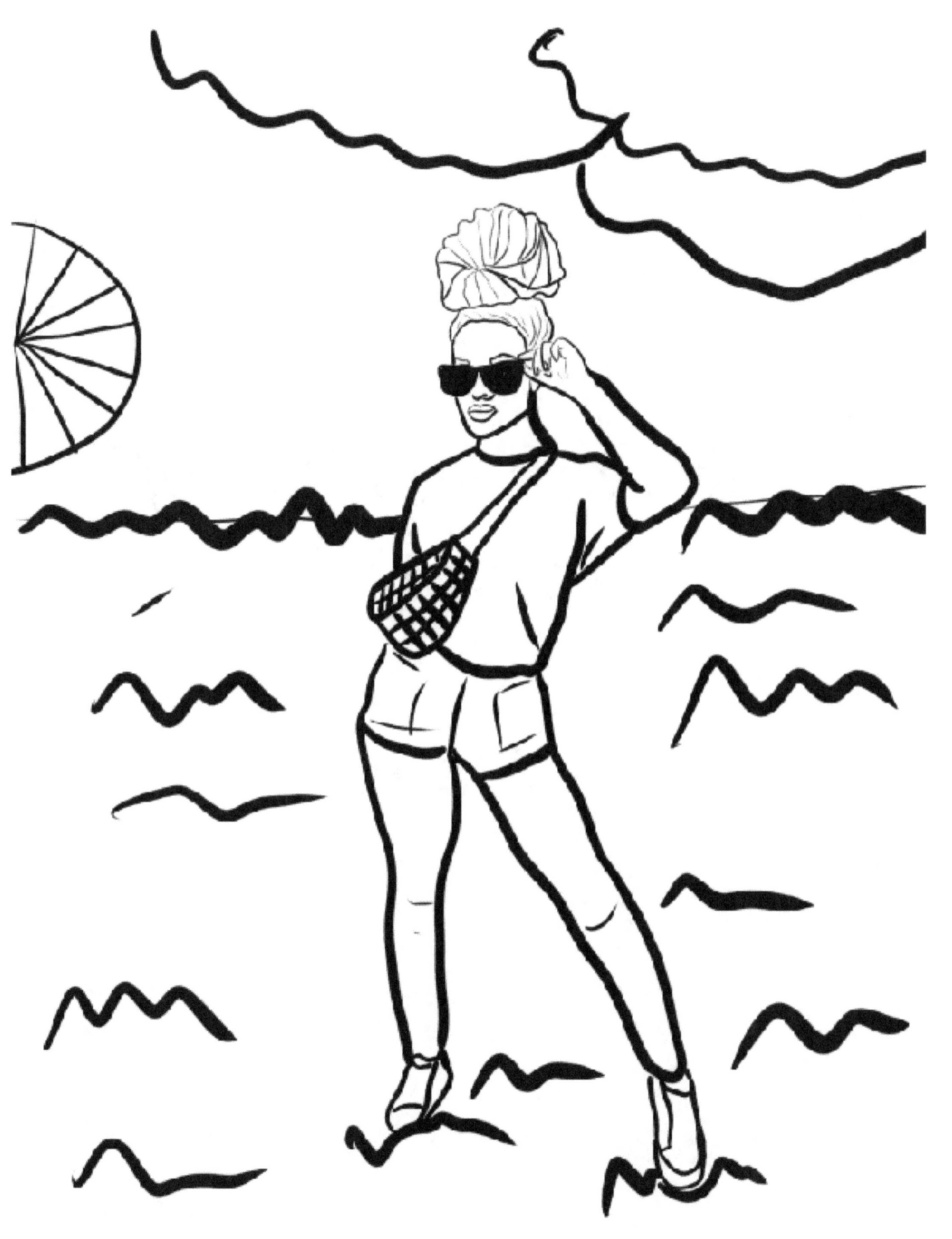

"You are capable of anything."

—Monet

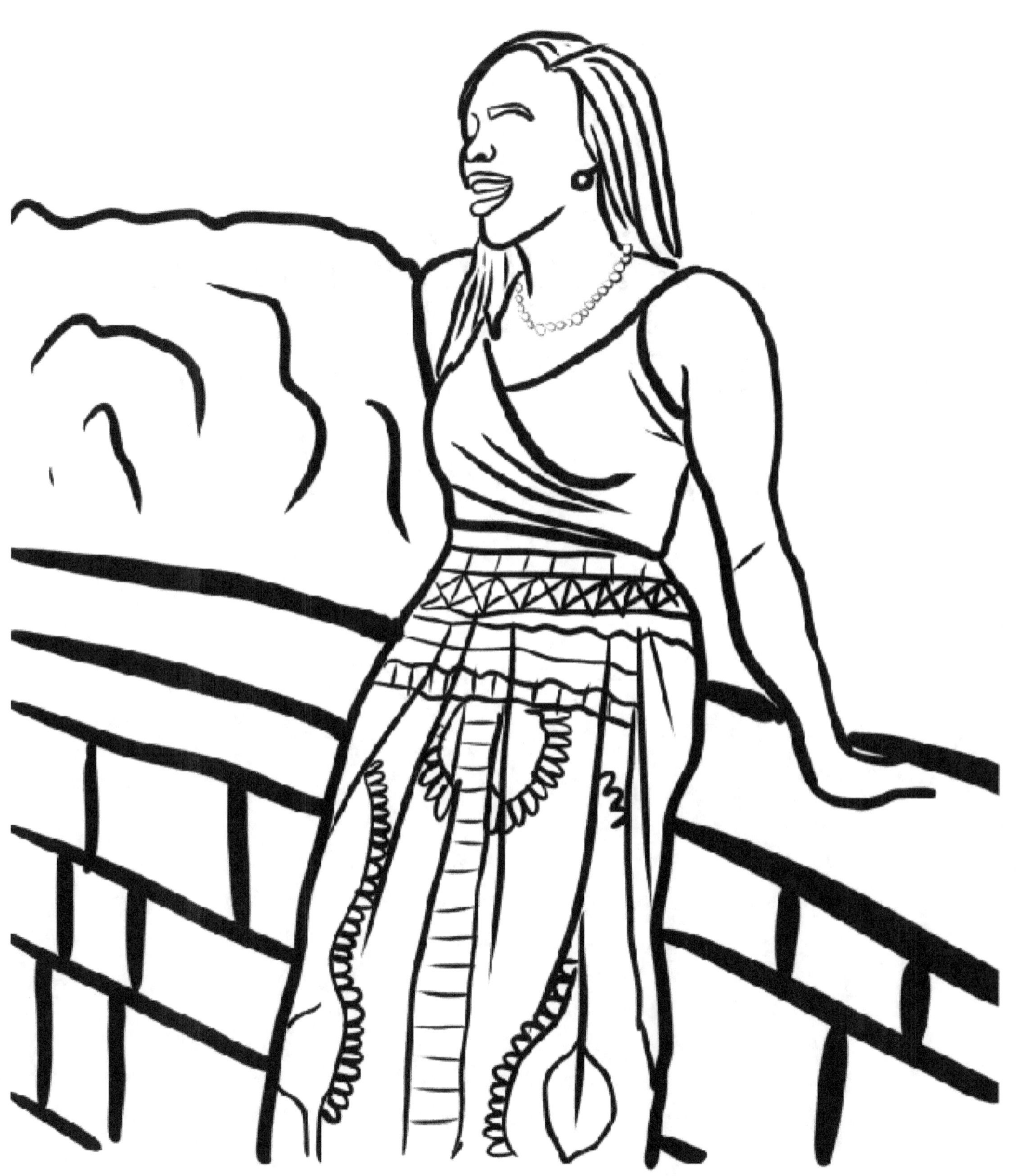

"Don't let the world silence you. Be loud and be proud."

—Naomi

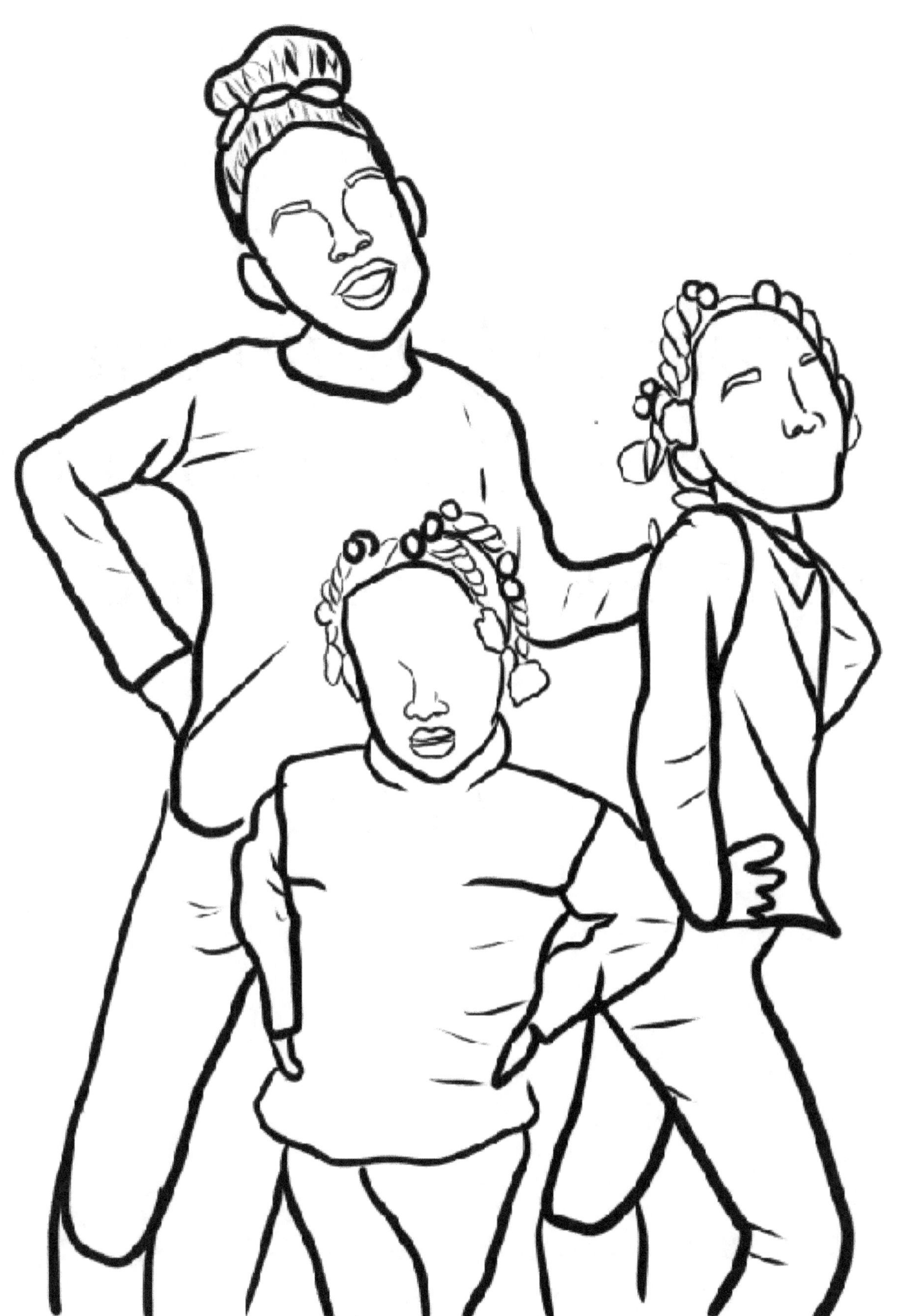

"*Your body is no one's property. You don't owe your body to anyone.*"

—*Naomi*

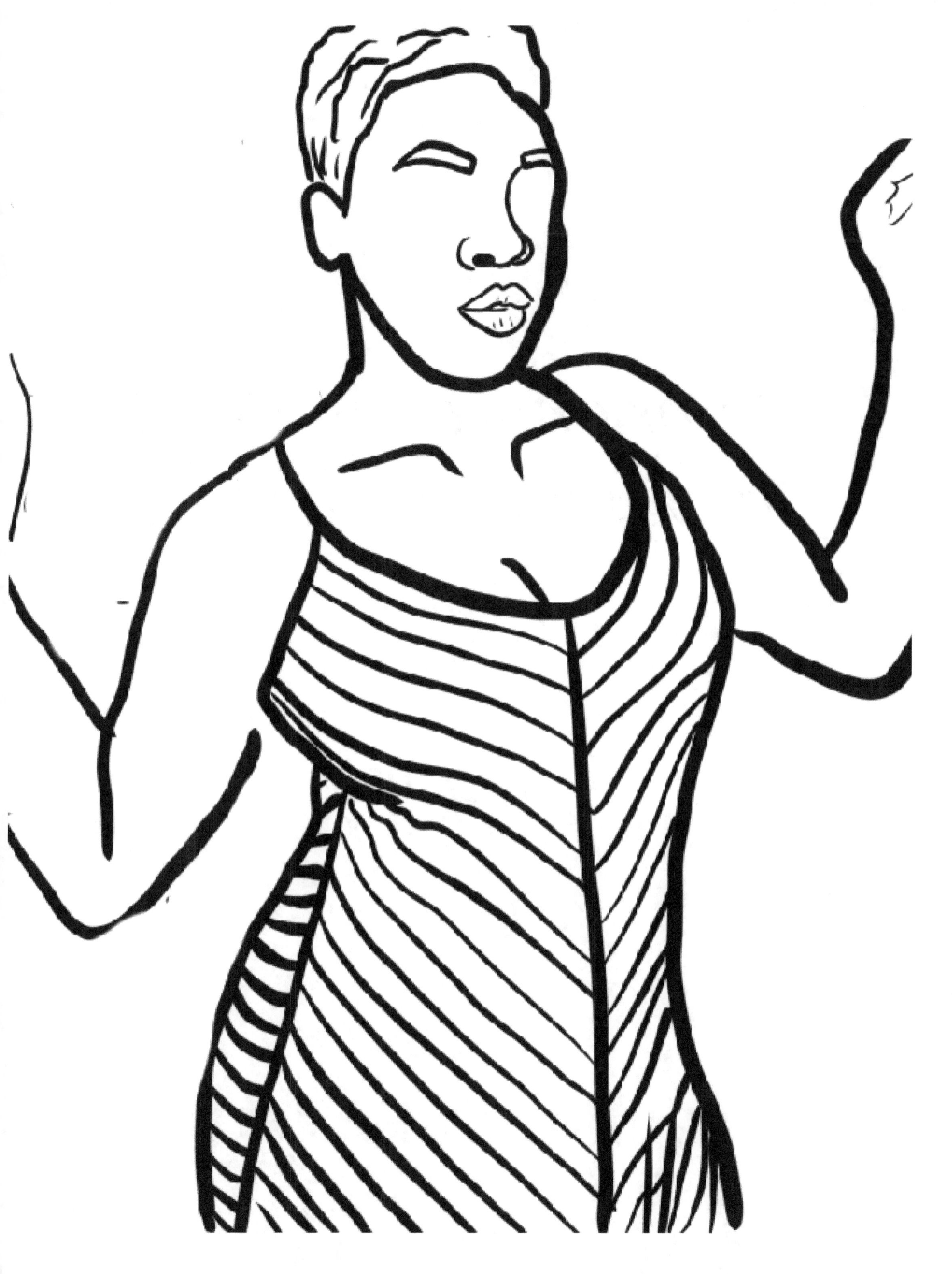

"*Work hard but don't let your work destroy you.*"

—*Naomi*

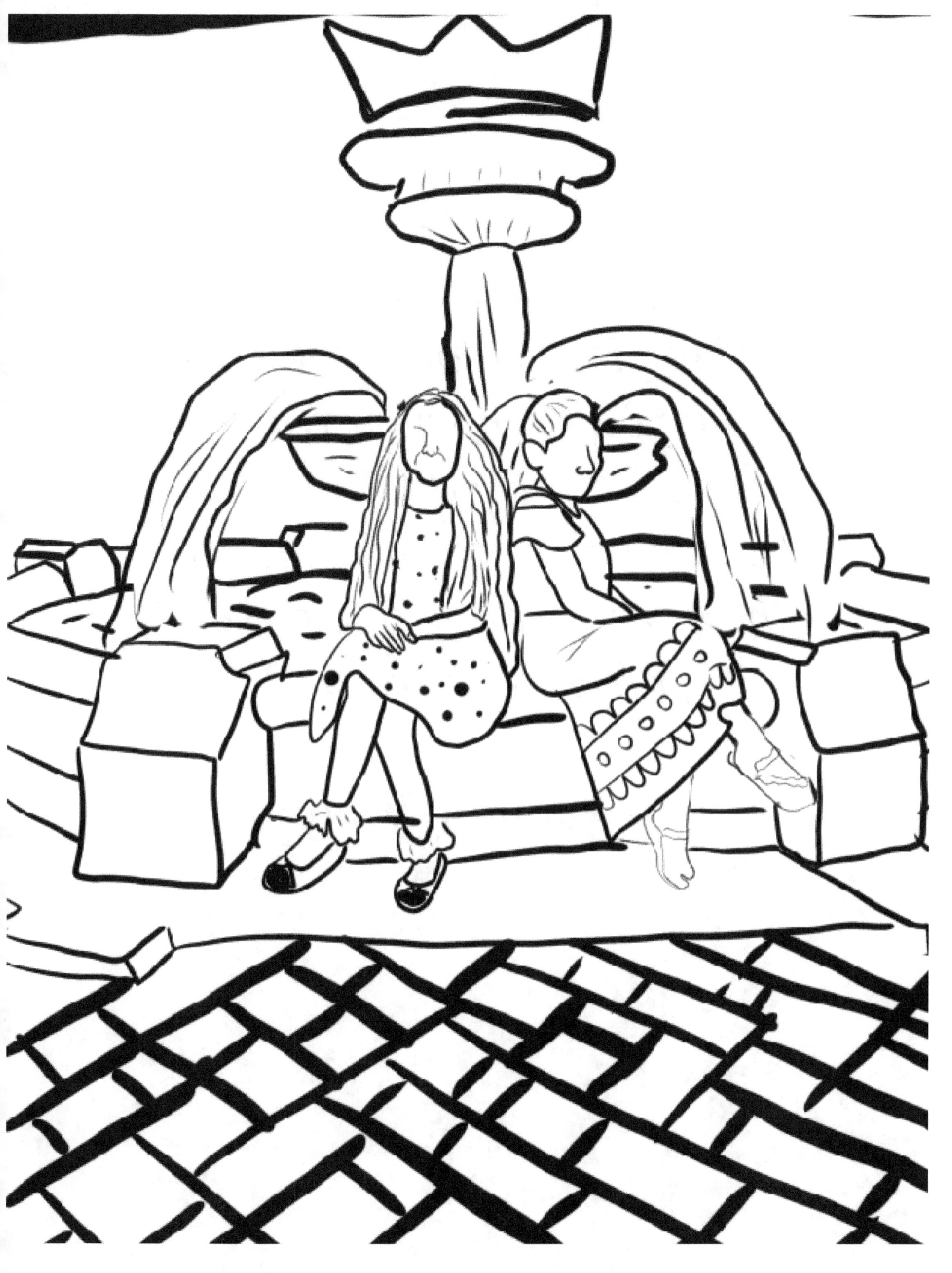

"There is someone who cares about you even when you think there isn't. Find faith in one person and communicate with them freely. Someone cares. I promise they do!"

—Naomi Winston

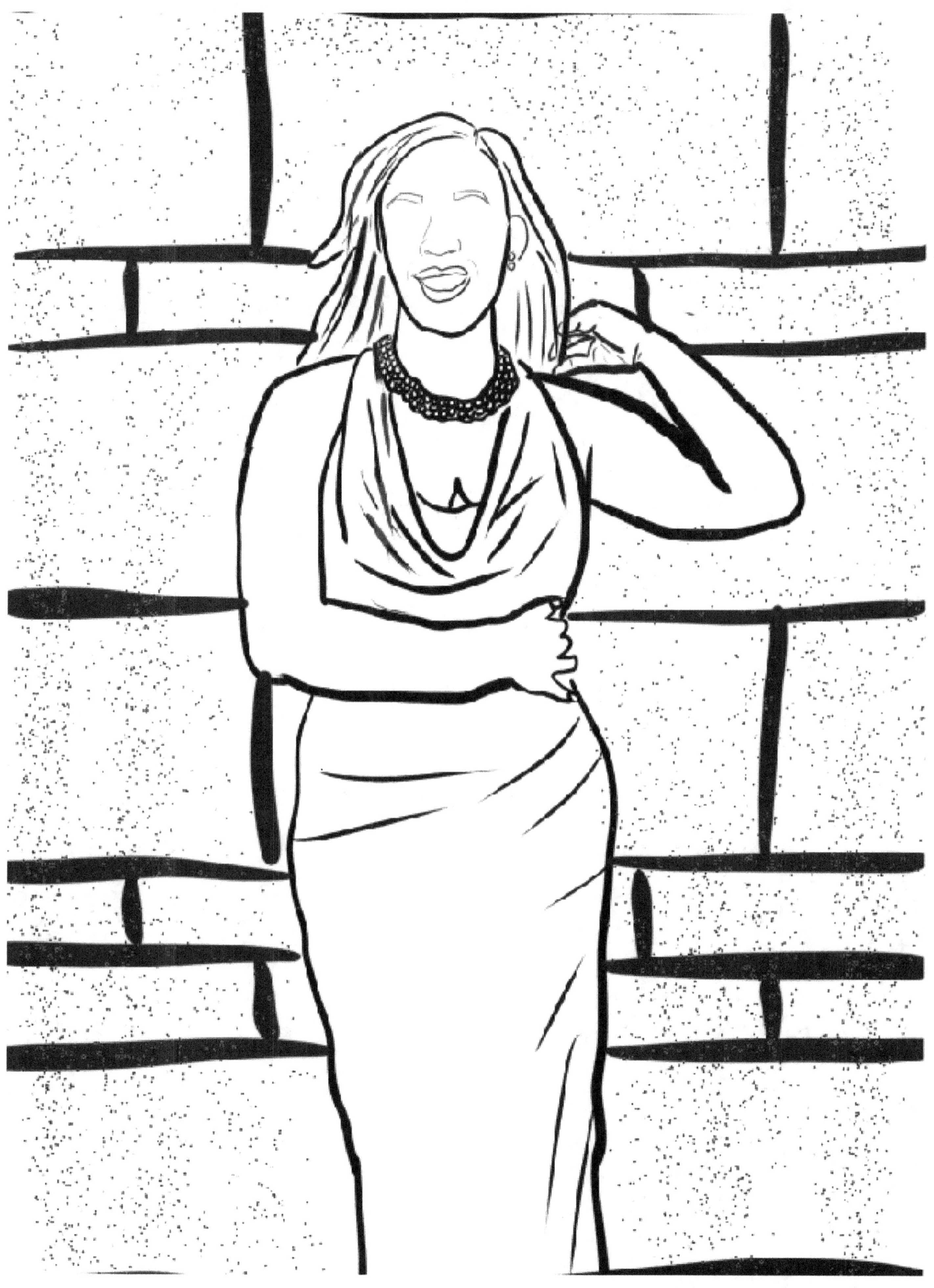

"*Your sisters are not your enemies.*"

—*Naomi*

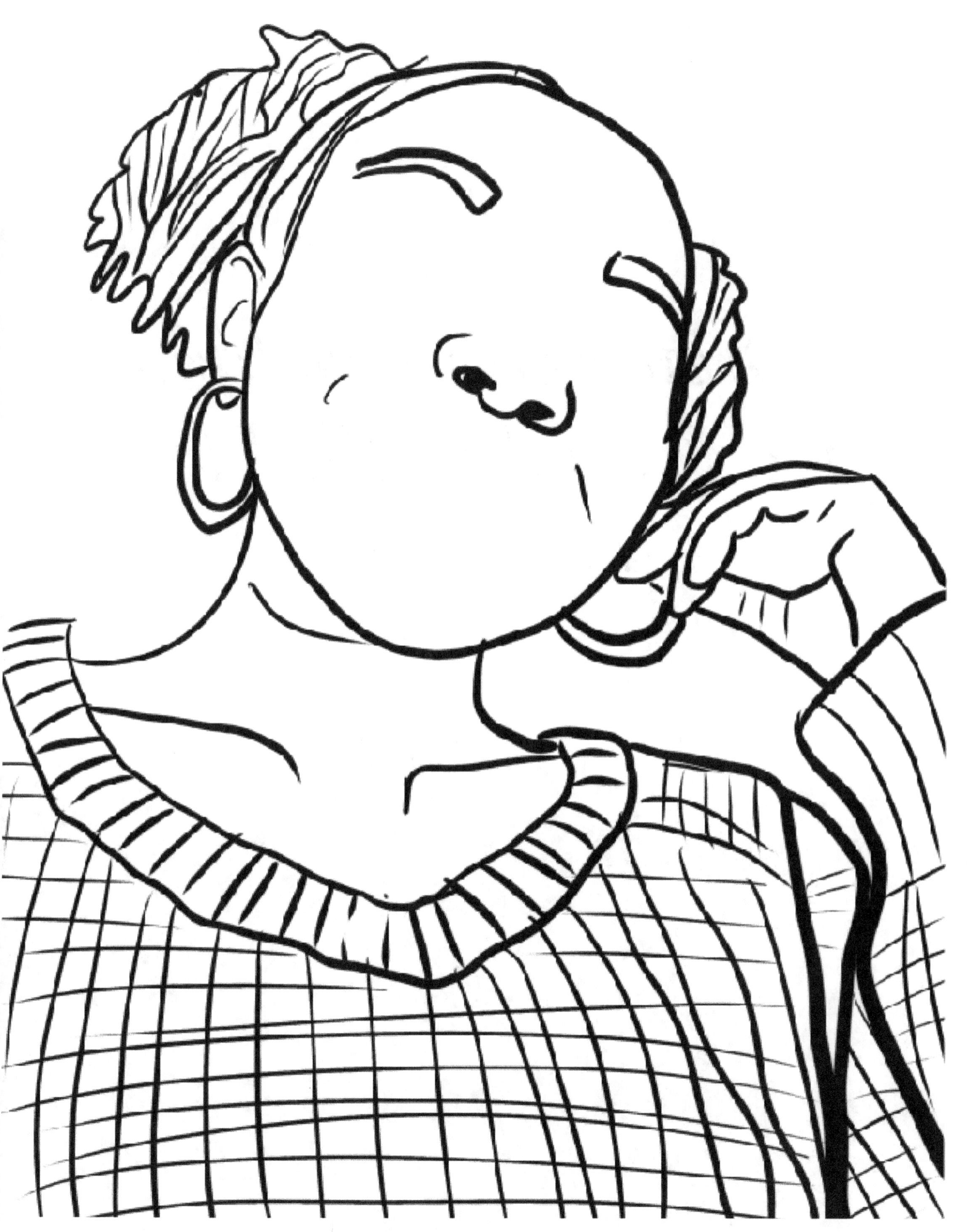

"*Drenched in Melanin and Kissed by the Sun-I am Light.*"

—*Alexis*

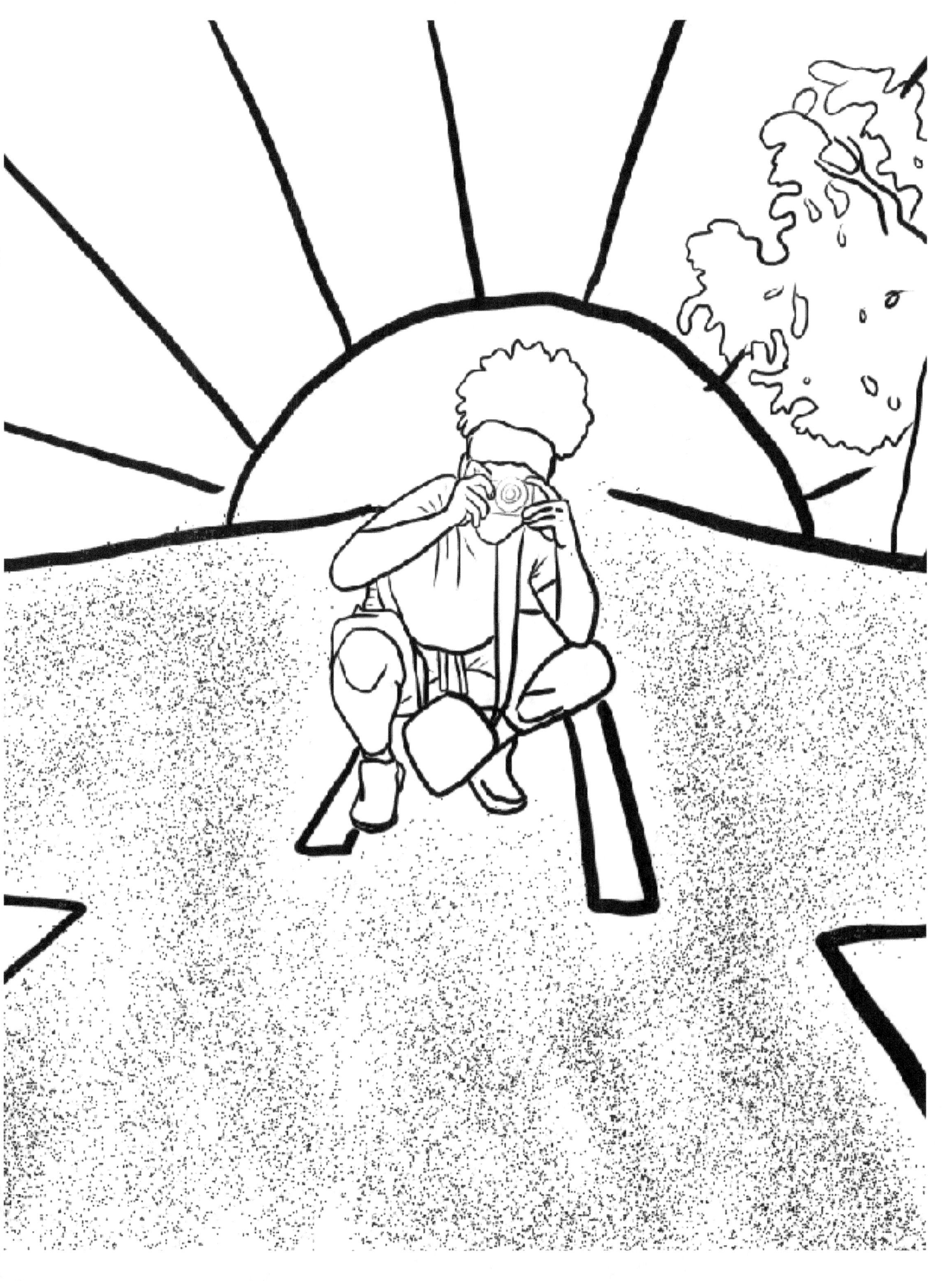

"My white professor thought my F was good enough, so I worked harder."

—Alexis

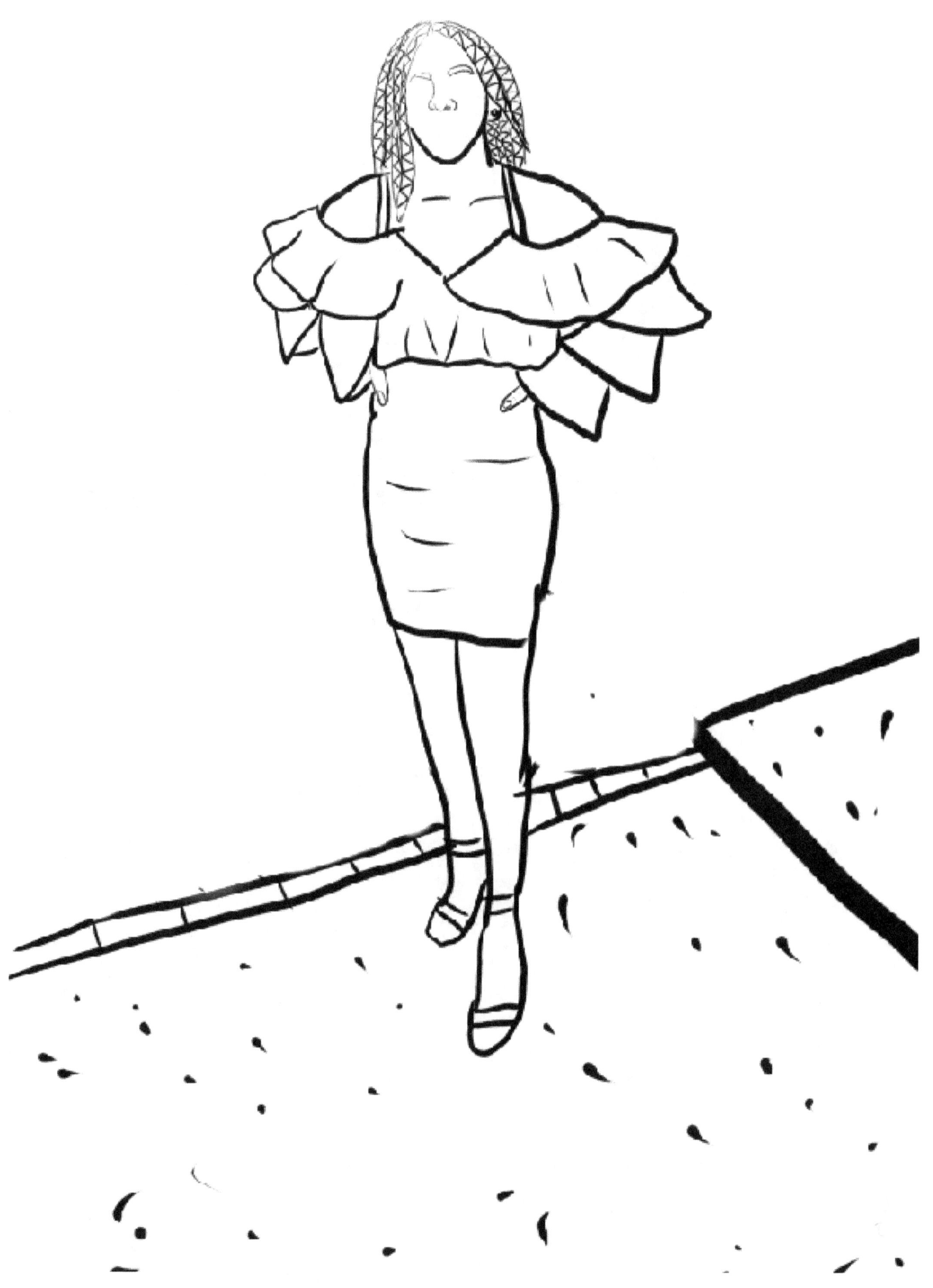

"Admit when you are wrong."

—Naomi

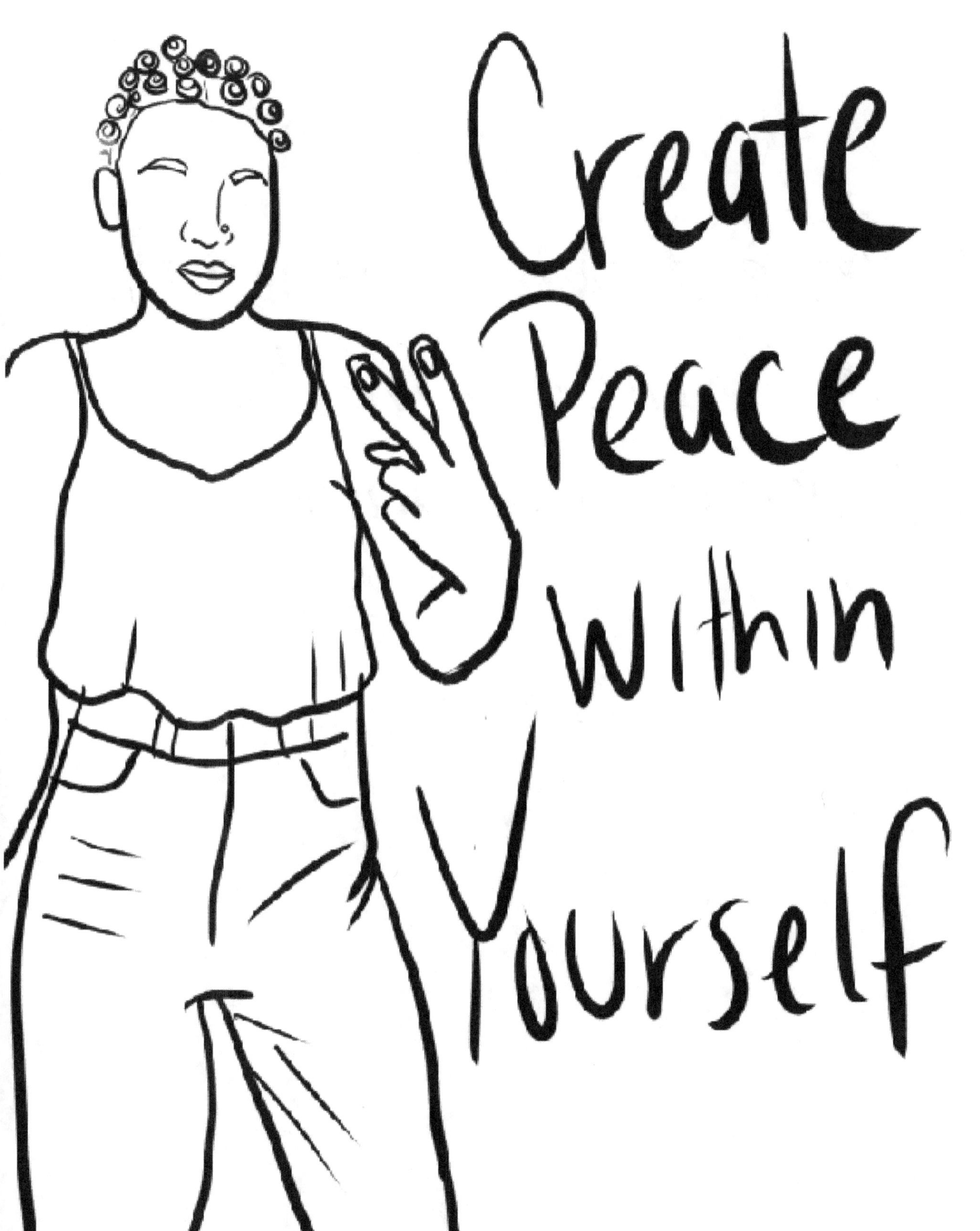

Create
Peace
Within
Yourself

*"Write down your goals
and watch how they
jump off the pages."*

—Naomi

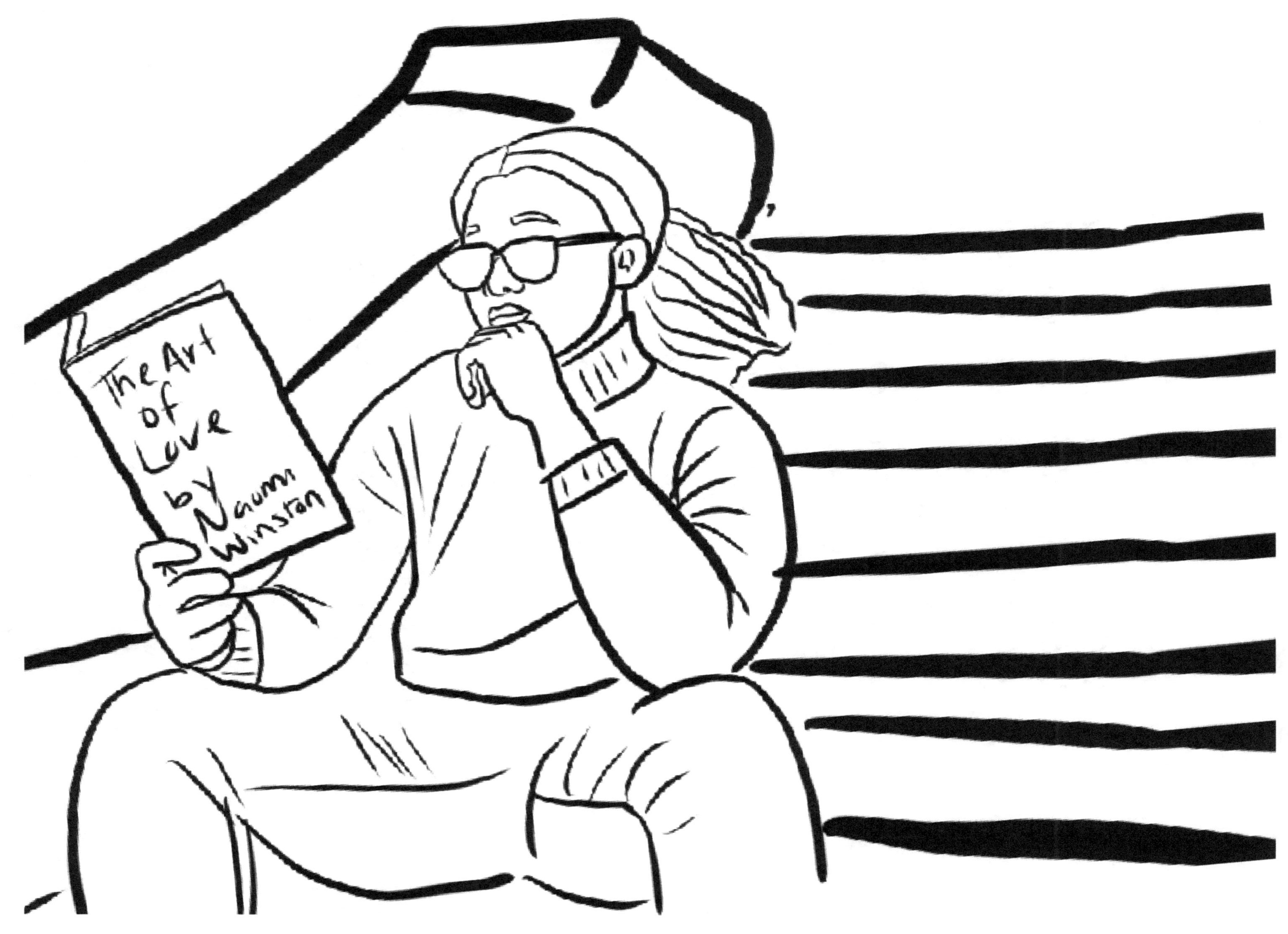

The Art
of
Love
by Naomi Winston

Little black girl you are beautiful.
Little black girl you are powerful.
Little black girl you are intelligent.

Your nose is not too big.
Your hair is not too nappy.
Your lips are not too puffy.

You are good enough.
You are beautiful enough.
You are intelligent enough.

You are enough.
You are loved.
You are respected.

-from a black girl who doesn't have to meet
you to know you're wonderful.

Write a note to your beautiful
black girl:

My name is Naomi Winston. I am a 19 year old black woman and did this coloring book for other young black women and girls like me.

I am the owner of Revolutionary Hearts Industries, LLC and through my company I work to spread representation for the underrepresented.

Little black girl, you deserve story book characters that look like you. You deserve coloring books that have features that you either have or will grow up to have. You deserve to know that you are beautiful.

Little black girl you were my heart and soul when I was creating this book. I hope that you know that there is another black girl in the world looking out for you.

If you want to learn more about me, my company, and my message Google (Revolutionary Hearts Industries).

You Are

Worth

IT!

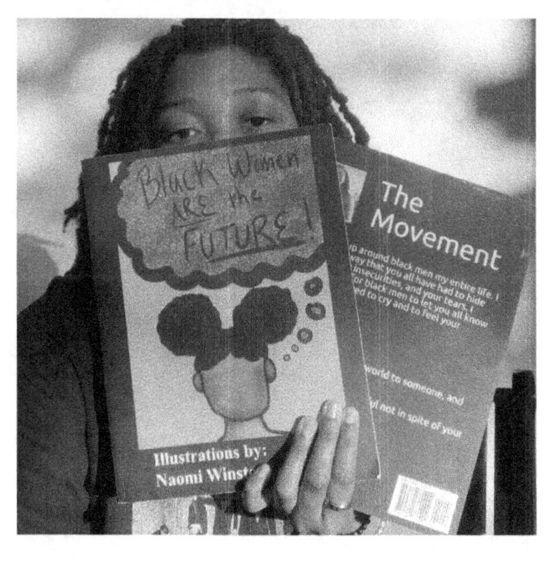

Creative Representation as a Movement for Change

Naomi Winston

Every day I am grateful for that day at the park that would lead me to publish this book. When I saw my beautiful little cousins express feelings of colorism at 5 and 6 years old it truly made me not only sad, but disappointed that I had not built a world where they felt safe, beautiful, and cherished for all the qualities that made them beautiful Black girls.

I told myself that I would never republish this book because I wanted it to stand as a testament to how I didn't know what I was doing (or literally anything about coloring books) but that I knew that you deserved to feel beautiful and affirmed through the safe space my work would create.

I may not have all the answers. I may not be able to magically change the world to treat you as it should in one day. However, best believe that it is my personal mission on this Earth to create a space where you can find the courage to not only love yourself but where you can be empowered to create space for others.

Remember, everything happens for a reason and you are everything,